CAME DOWN FROM HEAVEN, AND HE BRO

AND LAID BEFORE OUR EYES,

AND SAW THE PLATES, AND TH

THEREON; AND WE KNOW THAT IS BY THE GRACE OF GOD THE FATHER, AND OUR LORD JESUS CHRIST, THAT WE BEHELD AND BEAR RECORD THAT THESE THINGS ARE TRUE. AND IT IS MARVELOUS IN OUR EYES. NEVERTHELESS, THE VOICE OF THE LORD COMMANDED US THAT WE SHOULD BEAR RECORD OF IT; WHEREFORE, TO BE OBEDIENT UNTO THE COMMANDMENTS OF GOD, WE BEAR TESTIMONY OF THESE THINGS. AND WE KNOW THAT IF WE ARE FAITHFUL IN CHRIST, WE SHALL RID OUR GARMENTS OF THE BLOOD OF ALL MEN, AND BE FOUND SPOTLESS BEFORE THE JUDGMENT-SEAT OF CHRIST, AND SHALL DWELL WITH HIM ETERNALLY IN THE HEAVENS. AND THE HONOR BE TO THE FATHER, AND TO THE SON, AND TO THE HOLY GHOST, WHICH IS ONE GOD. AMEN.

OLIVER COWDERY

DAVID WHITMER

MARTIN HARRIS

Book of Mormon Comics

Our Goal:
Make the scriptures more accessible and more enjoyable for all ages.

We created these comics to make The Book of Mormon more appealing to younger readers. We want everyone to enjoy reading The Book of Mormon, not just to spend time reading, but to *want* to spend time reading. We want readers to better remember what they read so they can better apply its lessons to their lives. We believe that graphic novel design helps with all of our hopes. Readers of any age can relate to the story as it is brought to life, word-for-word, through art.

A thought on forming a habit: did you know that making a good-habit more *enjoyable* will help someone stick with it even after some artificial enjoyment is taken away? We hope these comics will help you form one of the best habits—reading God's word every day.

Characters

Lehi: The prophet and father who leads his family out of Jerusalem when commanded by the Lord.

Sariah: Wife to Lehi, she follows him into the wilderness.

Laman: The oldest son of Lehi and Sariah, he often doubts his father and the Lord.

Lemuel: The second oldest son of Lehi and Sariah, he usually follows Laman.

Sam: The third son of Lehi and Sariah, more willing to listen to his father than his older brothers.

Nephi: The fourth and youngest son of Lehi and Sariah. He trusts God, though he often wants to know for himself as well.

Laban: A prominent citizen/leader of Jerusalem. The keeper of the brass plates.

Zoram: A trusted servant of Laban who has faith in the Lord.

Ishmael: A contemporary of Lehi, who also lived in or near the city of Jerusalem. He is the father of a large family.

Why Blue Words?

We have done our best to be true to the text while still giving you an amazing graphic novel. There are a few times where words have been repeated or slightly changed in order to create a speech bubble. Any words you see in blue are, in our opinion, justified by the text, but are changed for grammatical purposes. This should allow for better flow while reading. Examples are limited, but you will see this on a few pages. Most changes are made to pronouns. Example: Changing "he" to "you."

An account of Lehi and his wife Sariah, and his four sons, being called, (beginning at the eldest) Laman, Lemuel, Sam, and Nephi. The Lord warns Lehi to depart out of the land of Jerusalem, because he prophesieth unto the people concerning their iniquity and they seek to destroy his life. He taketh three days' journey into the wilderness with his family. Nephi taketh his brethren and returneth to the land of Jerusalem after the record of the Jews. The account of their sufferings. They take the daughters of Ishmael to wife. They take their families and depart into the wilderness. Their sufferings and afflictions in the wilderness. The course of their travels. They come to the large waters. Nephi's brethren rebel against him. He confoundeth them, and buildeth a ship. They call the name of the place Bountiful. They cross the large waters into the promised land, and so forth. This is according to the account of Nephi; or in other words, I, Nephi, wrote this record.

I, NEPHI, HAVING BEEN BORN OF GOODLY PARENTS, THEREFORE I WAS TAUGHT SOMEWHAT IN ALL THE LEARNING OF MY FATHER; AND HAVING SEEN MANY AFFLICTIONS IN THE COURSE OF MY DAYS, NEVERTHELESS, HAVING BEEN HIGHLY FAVORED OF THE LORD IN ALL MY DAYS; YEA, HAVING HAD A GREAT KNOWLEDGE OF THE GOODNESS AND THE MYSTERIES OF GOD, THEREFORE I MAKE A RECORD OF MY PROCEEDINGS IN MY DAYS.
YEA, I MAKE A RECORD IN THE LANGUAGE OF MY FATHER, WHICH CONSISTS OF THE LEARNING OF THE JEWS AND THE LANGUAGE OF THE EGYPTIANS.
AND I KNOW THAT THE RECORD WHICH I MAKE IS TRUE;
AND I MAKE IT WITH MINE OWN HAND;
AND I MAKE IT ACCORDING TO MY KNOWLEDGE.
FOR IT CAME TO PASS IN THE COMMENCEMENT OF THE FIRST YEAR OF THE REIGN OF ZEDEKIAH, KING OF JUDAH, (MY FATHER,LEHI, HAVING DWELT AT JERUSALEM IN ALL HIS DAYS);
AND IN THAT SAME YEAR THERE CAME MANY PROPHETS, PROPHESYING UNTO THE PEOPLE THAT THEY MUST REPENT, OR THE GREAT CITY JERUSALEM MUST BE DESTROYED.
WHEREFORE IT CAME TO PASS THAT MY FATHER, LEHI, AS HE WENT FORTH PRAYED UNTO THE LORD, YEA, EVEN WITH ALL HIS HEART, IN BEHALF OF HIS PEOPLE.

AND IT CAME TO PASS AS HE PRAYED UNTO THE LORD, THERE CAME A PILLAR OF FIRE AND DWELT UPON A ROCK BEFORE HIM;
AND HE SAW AND HEARD MUCH;
AND BECAUSE OF THE THINGS WHICH HE SAW AND HEARD HE DID QUAKE AND TREMBLE EXCEEDINGLY.
AND IT CAME TO PASS THAT HE RETURNED TO HIS OWN HOUSE AT JERUSALEM;
AND HE CAST HIMSELF UPON HIS BED, BEING OVERCOME WITH THE SPIRIT AND THE THINGS WHICH HE HAD SEEN.
AND BEING THUS OVERCOME WITH THE SPIRIT, HE WAS CARRIED AWAY IN A VISION, EVEN THAT HE SAW THE HEAVENS OPEN,
AND HE THOUGHT HE SAW GOD SITTING UPON HIS THRONE, SURROUNDED WITH NUMBERLESS CONCOURSES OF ANGELS IN THE ATTITUDE OF SINGING AND PRAISING THEIR GOD.

AND IT CAME TO PASS THAT HE SAW ONE DESCENDING OUT OF THE MIDST OF HEAVEN, AND HE BEHELD THAT HIS LUSTER WAS ABOVE THAT OF THE SUN AT NOON-DAY.
AND HE ALSO SAW TWELVE OTHERS FOLLO HIM, AND THEIR BRIGHTNESS DID EXCEED THA OF THE STARS IN THE FIRMAMENT.
AND THEY CAME DOWN AND WENT FORTH UPON THE FACE OF THE EARTH;
AND THE FIRST CAME AND STOOD BEFORE MY FATHER, AND GAVE UNTO HIM A BOOK, AND BADE HIM THAT HE SHOULD READ.
AND IT CAME TO PASS THAT AS HE READ, HE WAS FILLED WITH THE SPIRIT OF THE LORD.
AND HE READ, SAYING: WO, WO, UNTO JERUSALEM, FOR I HAVE SEEN THINE ABOMINATIONS! YEA, AND MANY THINGS DID MY FATHER READ CONCERNING JERUSALEM—THAT IT SHOULD BE DESTROYED, AND THE INHABITANTS THEREOF; MANY SHOULD PERISH BY THE SWORD, AND MANY SHOULD BE CARRIED AWAY CAPTIVE INTO BABYLON.

D IT CAME TO PASS THAT WHEN MY FATHER D READ AND SEEN MANY GREAT AND MARVE- OUS THINGS, HE DID EXCLAIM MANY THINGS NTO THE LORD; SUCH AS: GREAT AND MARVE- LOUS ARE THY WORKS, O LORD GOD ALMIGHTY! THY THRONE IS HIGH IN THE HEAVENS, AND THY POWER, AND GOODNESS, AND MERCY ARE OVER ALL THE INHABITANTS OF THE EARTH; AND, BE- CAUSE THOU ART MERCIFUL, THOU WILT NOT SUFFER THOSE WHO COME UNTO THEE THAT THEY SHALL PERISH!
AND AFTER THIS MANNER WAS THE LANGUAGE OF MY FATHER IN THE PRAISING OF HIS GOD; FOR HIS SOUL DID REJOICE, AND HIS WHOLE HEART WAS FILLED, BECAUSE OF THE THINGS WHICH HE HAD SEEN, YEA, WHICH THE LORD HAD SHOWN UNTO HIM.
AND NOW I, NEPHI, DO NOT MAKE A CCOUNT OF THE THINGS WHICH MY FATHER HATH WRITTEN, FOR HE HATH WRITTEN MANY THINGS WHICH HE SAW IN VISIONS AND IN DREAMS; AND HE ALSO HATH WRI- TTEN MANY THINGS WHICH HE PROPHESIED AND SPAKE UNTO HIS CHILDREN, OF WHICH I SHALL NOT MAKE A FULL ACCOUNT.
BUT I SHALL MAKE AN ACCOUNT OF MY PROCEEDINGS IN MY DAYS. BEHOLD, I MAKE AN ABRIDGMENT OF THE RECORD OF MY FATHER, UPON PLATES WHICH I HAVE MADE WITH MINE OWN HANDS; WHEREFORE, AFTER I HAVE ABRIDGED THE RECORD OF MY FATHER THEN WILL I MAKE AN AC- COUNT OF MINE OWN LIFE.
THEREFORE, I WOULD THAT YE SHOULD KNOW, THAT AFTER THE LORD HAD SHOWN SO MANY MARVELOUS THINGS UNTO MY FATHER, LEHI, YEA, CONCERNING THE DESTRUCTION OF JERU- SALEM, BEHOLD HE WENT FORTH AMONG THE PEOPLE, AND BEGAN TO PROPHESY AND TO DECLARE UNTO THEM CONCERNING THE THINGS WHICH HE HAD BOTH SEEN AND HEARD.

AND IT CAME TO PASS THAT THE JEWS DID MOCK HIM BECAUSE OF THE THINGS WHICH HE TESTIFIED OF THEM; FOR HE TRULY TESTIFIED OF THEIR WICKEDNESS AND THEIR ABOMINATIONS; AND HE TESTIFIED THAT THE THINGS WHICH HE SAW AND HEARD, AND ALSO THE THINGS WHICH HE READ IN THE BOOK, MANIFESTED PLAINLY OF THE COMING OF A MESSIAH, AND ALSO THE REDEMPTION OF THE WORLD.
AND WHEN THE JEWS HEARD THESE THINGS THEY WERE ANGRY WITH HIM; YEA, EVEN AS WITH THE PROPHETS OF OLD, WHOM THEY HAD CAST OUT, AND STONED, AND SLAIN;
AND THEY ALSO SOUGHT HIS LIFE, THAT THEY MIGHT TAKE IT AWAY.
BUT BEHOLD, I, NEPHI, WILL SHOW UNTO YOU THAT THE TENDER MERCIES OF THE LORD ARE OVER ALL THOSE WHOM HE HATH CHOSEN, BECAUSE OF THEIR FAITH, TO MAKE THEM MIGHTY EVEN UNTO THE POWER OF DELIVERANCE.

FOR BEHOLD, IT CAME TO PASS THAT THE LORD SPAKE UNTO MY FATHER, YEA, EVEN IN A DREAM, AND SAID UNTO HIM:
BLESSED ART THOU LEHI, BECAUSE OF THE THINGS WHICH THOU HAST DONE;
AND BECAUSE THOU HAST BEEN FAITHFUL AND DECLARED UNTO THIS PEOPLE THE THINGS WHICH I COMMANDED THEE, BEHOLD, THEY SEEK TO TAKE AWAY THY LIFE.
AND IT CAME TO PASS THAT THE LORD COMMANDED MY FATHER, EVEN IN A DREAM, THAT HE SHOULD TAKE HIS FAMILY AND DEPART INTO THE WILDERNESS.
TAKE YOUR FAMILY AND DEPART INTO THE WILDERNESS

AND IT CAME TO PASS THAT HE WAS OBEDIENT UNTO THE WORD OF THE LORD, WHEREFORE HE DID AS THE LORD COMMANDED HIM.
AND IT CAME TO PASS THAT HE DEPARTED INTO THE WILDERNESS. AND HE LEFT HIS HOUSE, AND THE LAND OF HIS INHERITANCE,

...AND HIS GOLD, AND HIS SILVER,
...AND HIS PRECIOUS THINGS,...
AND TOOK NOTHING WITH HIM, SAVE IT WERE HIS FAMILY, AND PROVISIONS, AND TENTS, AND DEPARTED INTO THE WILDERNESS.

AND HE CAME DOWN BY THE BORDERS NEAR THE SHORE OF THE RED SEA;
AND HE TRAVELED IN THE WILDERNESS IN THE BORDERS WHICH ARE NEARER THE RED SEA;
AND HE DID TRAVEL IN THE WILDERNESS WITH HIS FAMILY, WHICH CONSISTED OF

MY MOTHER, SARIAH,
AND MY ELDER BROTHERS, WHO WERE...
LAMAN,
LEMUEL,
AND SAM.
AND IT CAME TO PASS THAT WHEN HE HAD TRAVELED THREE DAYS IN THE WILDERNESS,...

HE PITCHED HIS TENT IN A VALLEY BY THE SIDE OF A RIVER OF WATER.
AND IT CAME TO PASS THAT HE BUILT AN ALTAR OF STONES, AND MADE AN OFFERING UNTO THE LORD,
AND GAVE THANKS UNTO THE LORD OUR GOD.

AND IT CAME TO PASS THAT HE CALLED THE NAME OF THE RIVER, LAMAN, AND IT EMPTIED INTO THE RED SEA; AND THE VALLEY WAS IN THE BORDERS NEAR THE MOUTH THEREOF.
AND WHEN MY FATHER SAW THAT THE WATERS OF THE RIVER EMPTIED INTO THE FOUNTAIN OF THE RED SEA, HE SPAKE UNTO LAMAN, SAYING:
O THAT THOU MIGHTEST BE LIKE UNTO THIS RIVER, CONTINUALLY RUNNING INTO THE FOUNTAIN OF ALL RIGHTEOUSNESS!
AND HE ALSO SPAKE UNTO LEMUEL:
O THAT THOU MIGHTEST BE LIKE UNTO THIS VALLEY, FIRM AND STEADFAST, AND IMMOVABLE IN KEEPING THE COMMANDMENTS OF THE LORD!
NOW THIS HE SPAKE BECAUSE OF THE STIFFNECKEDNESS OF LAMAN AND LEMUEL;

FOR BEHOLD THEY DID MURMUR IN MANY THINGS AGAINST THEIR FATHER, BECAUSE HE WAS A VISIONARY MAN,
AND HAD LED THEM OUT OF THE LAND OF JERUSALEM, TO LEAVE THE LAND OF THEIR INHERITANCE, AND THEIR GOLD, AND THEIR SILVER, AND THEIR PRECIOUS THINGS,
TO PERISH IN THE WILDERNESS.
AND THIS THEY SAID HE HAD DONE BECAUSE OF THE FOOLISH IMAGINATIONS OF HIS HEART.
AND THUS LAMAN AND LEMUEL, BEING THE ELDEST, DID MURMUR AGAINST THEIR FATHER. AND THEY DID MURMUR BECAUSE THEY KNEW NOT THE DEALINGS OF THAT GOD WHO HAD CREATED THEM. NEITHER DID THEY BELIEVE THAT JERUSALEM, THAT GREAT CITY, COULD BE DESTROYED ACCORDING TO THE WORDS OF THE PROPHETS.
AND THEY WERE LIKE UNTO THE JEWS WHO WERE AT JERUSALEM, WHO SOUGHT TO TAKE AWAY THE LIFE OF MY FATHER.

AND IT CAME TO PASS THAT MY FATHER DID SPEAK UNTO THEM IN THE VALLEY OF LEMUEL,
WITH POWER, BEING FILLED WITH THE SPIRIT,...
UNTIL THEIR FRAMES DID SHAKE BEFORE HIM.
AND HE DID CONFOUND THEM, THAT THEY DURST NOT UTTER AGAINST HIM;
WHEREFORE, THEY DID AS HE COMMANDED THEM.

AND MY FATHER DWELT IN A TENT.
AND IT CAME TO PASS THAT I, NEPHI, BEING EXCEEDINGLY YOUNG, NEVERTHELESS BEING LARGE IN STATURE,...
AND ALSO HAVING GREAT DESIRES TO KNOW OF THE MYSTERIES OF GOD,
WHEREFORE, I DID CRY UNTO THE LORD;

AND BEHOLD HE DID VISIT ME, AND DID SOFTEN MY HEART THAT I DID BELIEVE ALL THE WORDS WHICH HAD BEEN SPOKEN BY MY FATHER;
WHEREFORE, I DID NOT REBEL AGAINST HIM LIKE UNTO MY BROTHERS.
AND I SPAKE UNTO SAM, MAKING KNOWN UNTO HIM THE THINGS WHICH THE LORD HAD MANIFES-TED UNTO ME BY HIS HOLY SPIRIT.
AND IT CAME TO PASS THAT HE BELIEVED IN MY WORDS.
BUT, BEHOLD, LAMAN AND LEMUEL WOULD NOT HE-ARKEN UNTO MY WORDS;
AND BEING GRIEVED BECAUSE OF THE HARDNESS OF THEIR HEARTS...

I CRIED UNTO THE LORD FOR THEM. AND IT CAME TO PASS THAT THE LORD SPAKE UNTO ME, SAYING:
BLESSED ART THOU, NEPHI, BECAUSE OF THY FAITH, FOR THOU HAST SOUGHT ME DILIGENTLY, WITH LOWLINESS OF HEART.
AND INASMUCH AS YE SHALL KEEP MY COMMANDMENTS, YE SHALL PROSPER, AND SHALL BE LED TO A LAND OF PROMISE; YEA, EVEN A LAND WHICH I HAVE PREPARED FOR YOU; YEA, A LAND WHICH IS CHOICE ABOVE ALL OTHER LANDS.
AND INASMUCH AS THY BRETHREN SHALL REBEL AGAINST THEE, THEY SHALL BE CUT OFF FROM THE PRESENCE OF THE LORD.
AND INASMUCH AS THOU SHALT KEEP MY COMMANDMENTS, THOU SHALT BE MADE A RULER AND A TEACHER OVER THY BRETHREN.
FOR BEHOLD, IN THAT DAY THAT THEY SHALL REBEL AGAINST ME, I WILL CURSE THEM EVEN WITH A SORE CURSE, AND THEY SHALL HAVE NO POWER OVER THY SEED EXCEPT THEY SHALL REBEL AGAINST ME ALSO.
AND IF IT SO BE THAT THEY REBEL AGAINST ME, THEY SHALL BE A SCOURGE UNTO THY SEED, TO STIR THEM UP IN THE WAYS OF REMEMBRANCE.

AND IT CAME TO PASS THAT I, NEPHI, RETURNED FROM SPEAKING WITH THE LORD, TO THE TENT OF MY FATHER. AND IT CAME TO PASS THAT HE SPAKE UNTO ME, SAYING:
BEHOLD I HAVE DREAMED A DREAM, IN THE WHICH THE LORD HATH COMMANDED ME THAT THOU AND THY BRETHREN SHALL RETURN TO JERUSALEM.
FOR BEHOLD, LABAN HATH THE RECORD OF THE JEWS AND ALSO A GENEALOGY OF MY FOREFATHERS, AND THEY ARE ENGRAVEN UPON PLATES OF BRASS.
WHEREFORE, THE LORD HATH COMMANDED ME THAT THOU AND THY BROTHERS SHOULD GO UNTO THE HOUSE OF LABAN,
AND SEEK THE RECORDS, AND BRING THEM DOWN HITHER INTO THE WILDERNESS. AND NOW, BEHOLD THY BROTHERS MURMUR, SAYING IT IS A HARD THING WHICH I HAVE REQUIRED OF THEM;
BUT BEHOLD I HAVE NOT REQUIRED IT OF THEM, BUT IT IS A COMMANDMENT OF THE LORD.

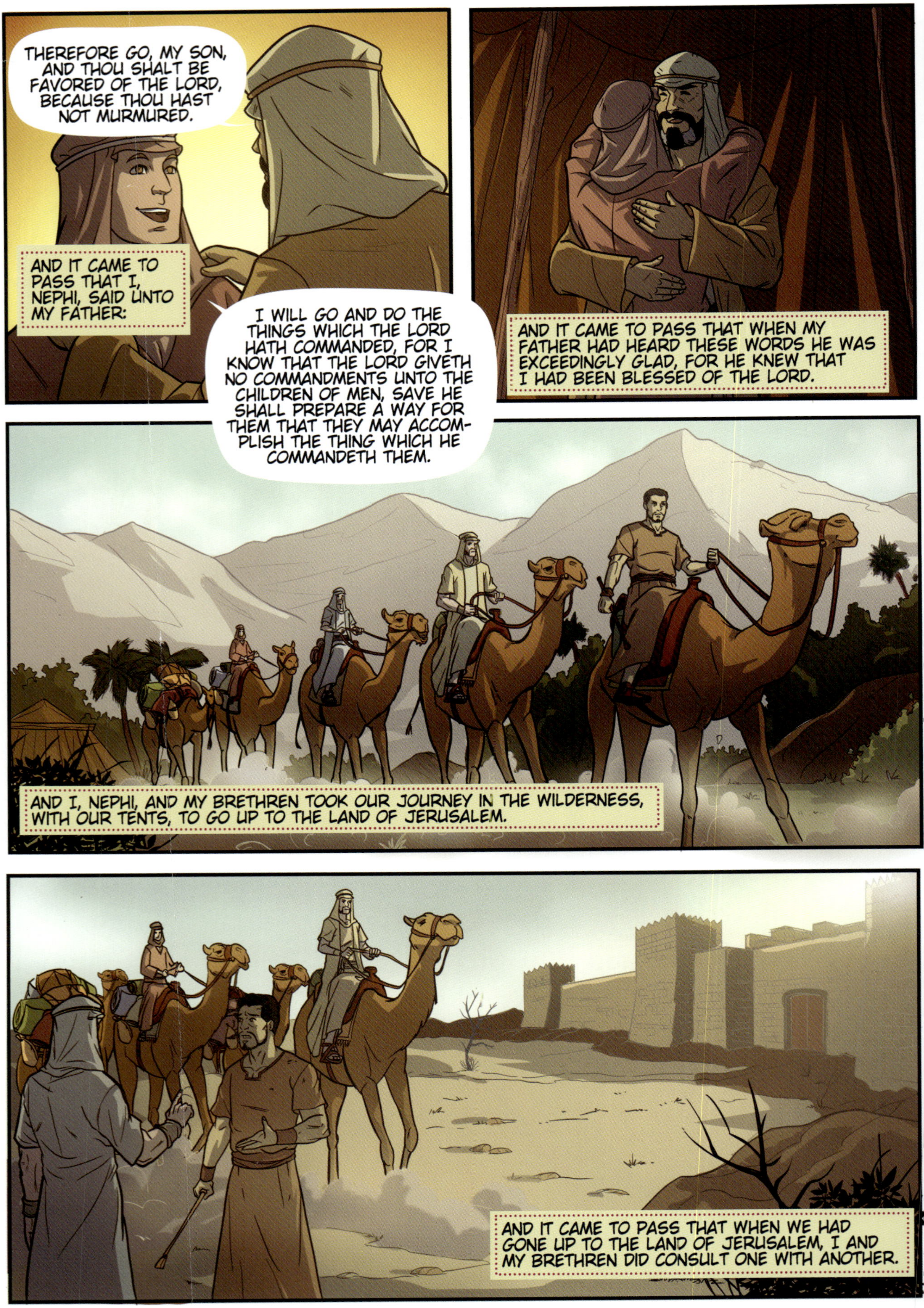

THEREFORE GO, MY SON, AND THOU SHALT BE FAVORED OF THE LORD, BECAUSE THOU HAST NOT MURMURED.
AND IT CAME TO PASS THAT I, NEPHI, SAID UNTO MY FATHER:
I WILL GO AND DO THE THINGS WHICH THE LORD HATH COMMANDED, FOR I KNOW THAT THE LORD GIVETH NO COMMANDMENTS UNTO THE CHILDREN OF MEN, SAVE HE SHALL PREPARE A WAY FOR THEM THAT THEY MAY ACCOMPLISH THE THING WHICH HE COMMANDETH THEM.
AND IT CAME TO PASS THAT WHEN MY FATHER HAD HEARD THESE WORDS HE WAS EXCEEDINGLY GLAD, FOR HE KNEW THAT I HAD BEEN BLESSED OF THE LORD.
AND I, NEPHI, AND MY BRETHREN TOOK OUR JOURNEY IN THE WILDERNESS, WITH OUR TENTS, TO GO UP TO THE LAND OF JERUSALEM.
AND IT CAME TO PASS THAT WHEN WE HAD GONE UP TO THE LAND OF JERUSALEM, I AND MY BRETHREN DID CONSULT ONE WITH ANOTHER.

AND WE CAST LOTS...
WHO OF US SHOULD GO IN UNTO THE HOUSE OF LABAN.
AND IT CAME TO PASS THAT THE LOT FELL UPON LAMAN;
AND LAMAN WENT IN UNTO THE HOUSE OF LABAN,...
AND HE TALKED WITH HIM AS HE SAT IN HIS HOUSE.

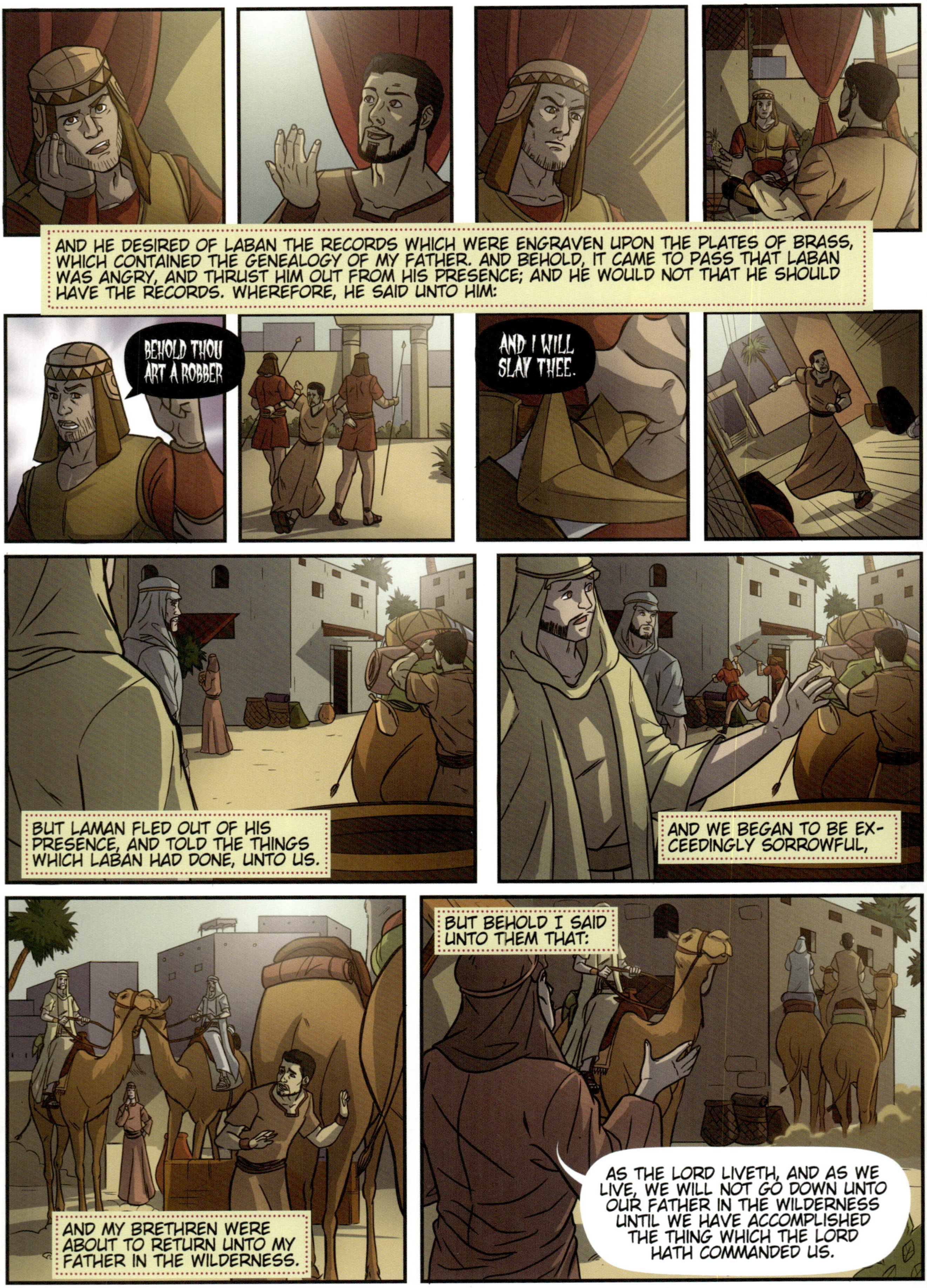
AND HE DESIRED OF LABAN THE RECORDS WHICH WERE ENGRAVEN UPON THE PLATES OF BRASS, WHICH CONTAINED THE GENEALOGY OF MY FATHER. AND BEHOLD, IT CAME TO PASS THAT LABAN WAS ANGRY, AND THRUST HIM OUT FROM HIS PRESENCE; AND HE WOULD NOT THAT HE SHOULD HAVE THE RECORDS. WHEREFORE, HE SAID UNTO HIM:
BEHOLD THOU ART A ROBBER
AND I WILL SLAY THEE.
BUT LAMAN FLED OUT OF HIS PRESENCE, AND TOLD THE THINGS WHICH LABAN HAD DONE, UNTO US.
AND WE BEGAN TO BE EXCEEDINGLY SORROWFUL,
AND MY BRETHREN WERE ABOUT TO RETURN UNTO MY FATHER IN THE WILDERNESS.
BUT BEHOLD I SAID UNTO THEM THAT:
AS THE LORD LIVETH, AND AS WE LIVE, WE WILL NOT GO DOWN UNTO OUR FATHER IN THE WILDERNESS UNTIL WE HAVE ACCOMPLISHED THE THING WHICH THE LORD HATH COMMANDED US.

WHEREFORE, LET US BE FAITHFUL IN KEEPING THE COMMANDMENTS OF THE LORD;
THEREFORE LET US GO DOWN TO THE LAND OF OUR FATHER'S INHERITANCE, FOR BEHOLD HE LEFT GOLD AND SILVER, AND ALL MANNER OF RICHES.
AND ALL THIS HE HATH DONE BECAUSE OF THE COMMANDMENTS OF THE LORD. FOR HE KNEW THAT JERUSALEM MUST BE DESTROYED, BECAUSE OF THE WICKEDNESS OF THE PEOPLE.
FOR BEHOLD, THEY HAVE REJECTED THE WORDS OF THE PROPHETS. WHEREFORE, IF MY FATHER SHOULD DWELL IN THE LAND AFTER HE HATH BEEN COMMANDED TO FLEE OUT OF THE LAND, BEHOLD, HE WOULD ALSO PERISH.
WHEREFORE, IT MUST NEEDS BE THAT HE FLEE OUT OF THE LAND. AND BEHOLD, IT IS WISDOM IN GOD THAT WE SHOULD OBTAIN THESE RECORDS, THAT WE MAY PRESERVE UNTO OUR CHILDREN THE LANGUAGE OF OUR FATHERS;
AND ALSO THAT WE MAY PRESERVE UNTO THEM THE WORDS WHICH HAVE BEEN SPOKEN BY THE MOUTH OF ALL THE HOLY PROPHETS, WHICH HAVE BEEN DELIVERED UNTO THEM BY THE SPIRIT AND POWER OF GOD, SINCE THE WORLD BEGAN, EVEN DOWN UNTO THIS PRESENT TIME.

AND IT CAME TO PASS THAT AFTER THIS MANNER OF LANGUAGE DID I PERSUADE MY BRETHREN, THAT THEY MIGHT BE FAITHFUL IN KEEPING THE COMMANDMENTS OF GOD. AND IT CAME TO PASS THAT WE WENT DOWN TO THE LAND OF OUR INHERITANCE,...
AND WE DID GATHER TOGETHER OUR GOLD, AND OUR SILVER, AND OUR PRECIOUS THINGS.
AND AFTER WE HAD GATHERED THESE THINGS TOGETHER, WE WENT UP AGAIN UNTO THE HOUSE OF LABAN.
AND IT CAME TO PASS THAT WE WENT IN UNTO LABAN,
AND DESIRED HIM THAT HE WOULD GIVE UNTO US THE RECORDS WHICH WERE ENGRAVEN UPON THE PLATES OF BRASS,
FOR WHICH WE WOULD GIVE UNTO HIM OUR GOLD,...
AND OUR SILVER,...
AND ALL OUR PRECIOUS THINGS.
AND IT CAME TO PASS THAT WHEN LABAN SAW OUR PROPERTY, AND THAT IT WAS EXCEEDINGLY GREAT, HE DID LUST AFTER IT,

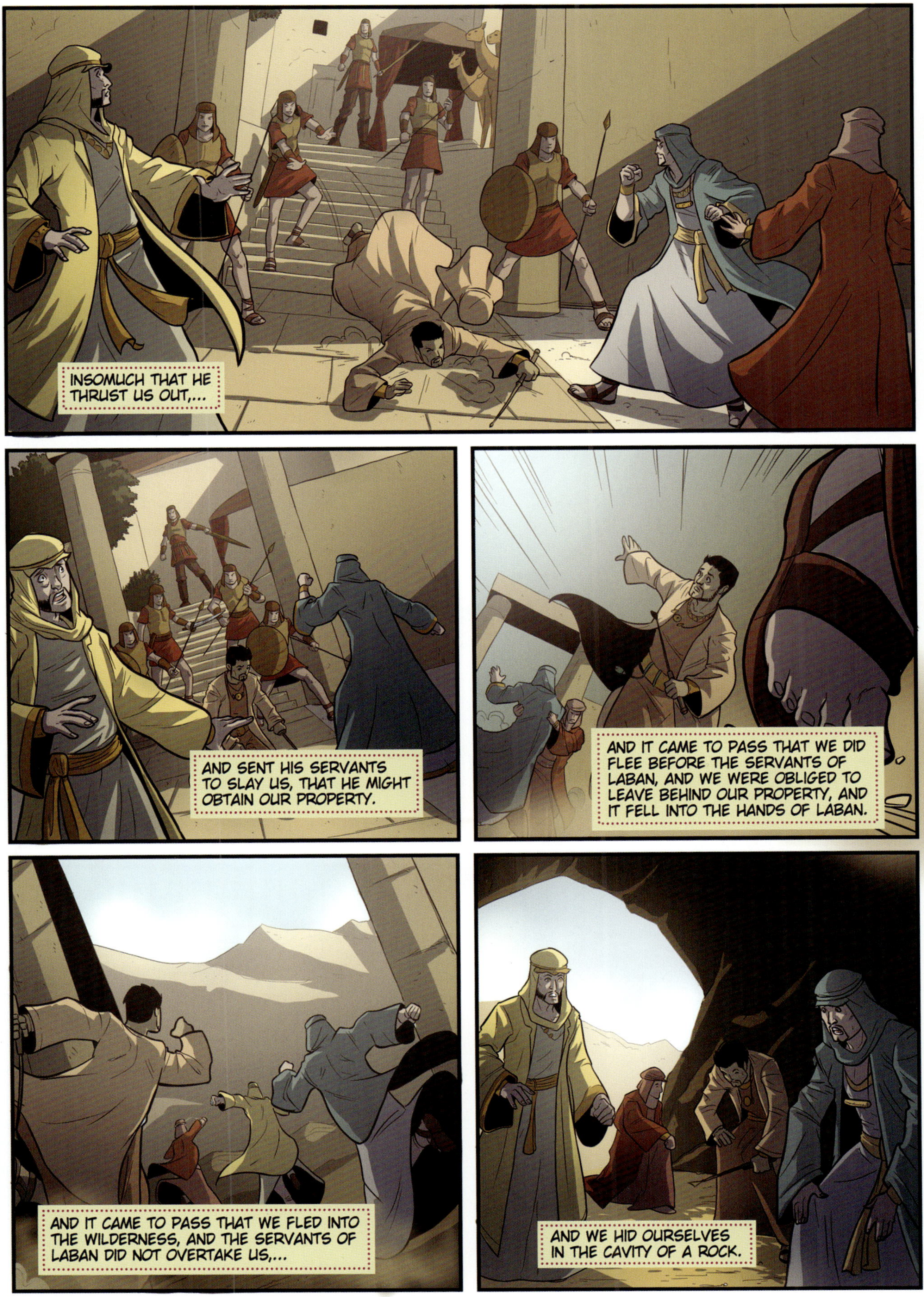
INSOMUCH THAT HE THRUST US OUT,...
AND SENT HIS SERVANTS TO SLAY US, THAT HE MIGHT OBTAIN OUR PROPERTY.
AND IT CAME TO PASS THAT WE DID FLEE BEFORE THE SERVANTS OF LABAN, AND WE WERE OBLIGED TO LEAVE BEHIND OUR PROPERTY, AND IT FELL INTO THE HANDS OF LABAN.
AND IT CAME TO PASS THAT WE FLED INTO THE WILDERNESS, AND THE SERVANTS OF LABAN DID NOT OVERTAKE US,...
AND WE HID OURSELVES IN THE CAVITY OF A ROCK.

AND IT CAME TO PASS THAT LAMAN WAS ANGRY WITH ME, AND ALSO WITH MY FATHER;
AND ALSO WAS LEMUEL, FOR HE HEARKENED UNTO THE WORDS OF LAMAN.
WHEREFORE LAMAN AND LEMUEL DID SPEAK MANY HARD WORDS UNTO US, THEIR YOUNGER BROTHERS, AND THEY DID SMITE US ....
EVEN WITH A ROD.
AND IT CAME TO PASS AS THEY SMOTE US WITH A ROD, BEHOLD, AN ANGEL OF THE LORD CAME

AND STOOD BEFORE THEM, AND HE SPAKE UNTO THEM, SAYING:
WHY DO YE SMITE YOUR YOUNGER BROTHER WITH A ROD?
KNOW YE NOT THAT THE LORD HATH CHOSEN HIM TO BE A RULER OVER YOU, AND THIS BECAUSE OF YOUR INIQUITIES?
BEHOLD YE SHALL GO UP TO JERUSALEM AGAIN, AND THE LORD WILL DELIVER LABAN INTO YOUR HANDS.
AND AFTER THE ANGEL HAD SPOKEN UNTO US, HE DEPARTED.
AND AFTER THE ANGEL HAD DEPARTED, LAMAN AND LEMUEL AGAIN BEGAN TO MURMUR, SAYING:
HOW IS IT POSSIBLE THAT THE LORD WILL DELIVER LABAN INTO OUR HANDS?
BEHOLD, HE IS A MIGHTY MAN, AND HE CAN COMMAND FIFTY,...
YEA, EVEN HE CAN SLAY FIFTY;
THEN WHY NOT US?
AND IT CAME TO PASS THAT I SPAKE UNTO MY BRETHREN, SAYING:
LET US GO UP AGAIN UNTO JERUSALEM,...

AND LET US BE FAITHFUL IN KEEPING THE COMMANDMENTS OF THE LORD; FOR BEHOLD HE IS MIGHTIER THAN ALL THE EARTH, THEN WHY NOT MIGHTIER THAN LABAN AND HIS FIFTY, YEA, OR EVEN THAN HIS TENS OF THOUSANDS?
THEREFORE LET US GO UP; LET US BE STRONG LIKE UNTO MOSES; FOR HE TRULY SPAKE UNTO THE WATERS OF THE RED SEA AND THEY DIVIDED HITHER AND THITHER,...
AND OUR FATHERS CAME THROUGH, OUT OF CAPTIVITY, ON DRY GROUND,
AND THE ARMIES OF PHARAOH DID FOLLOW AND WERE DROWNED IN THE WATERS OF THE RED SEA.
NOW BEHOLD YE KNOW THAT THIS IS TRUE; AND YE ALSO KNOW THAT AN ANGEL HATH SPOKEN UNTO YOU; WHEREFORE CAN YE DOUBT? LET US GO UP; THE LORD IS ABLE TO DELIVER US, EVEN AS OUR FATHERS, AND TO DESTROY LABAN, EVEN AS THE EGYPTIANS.

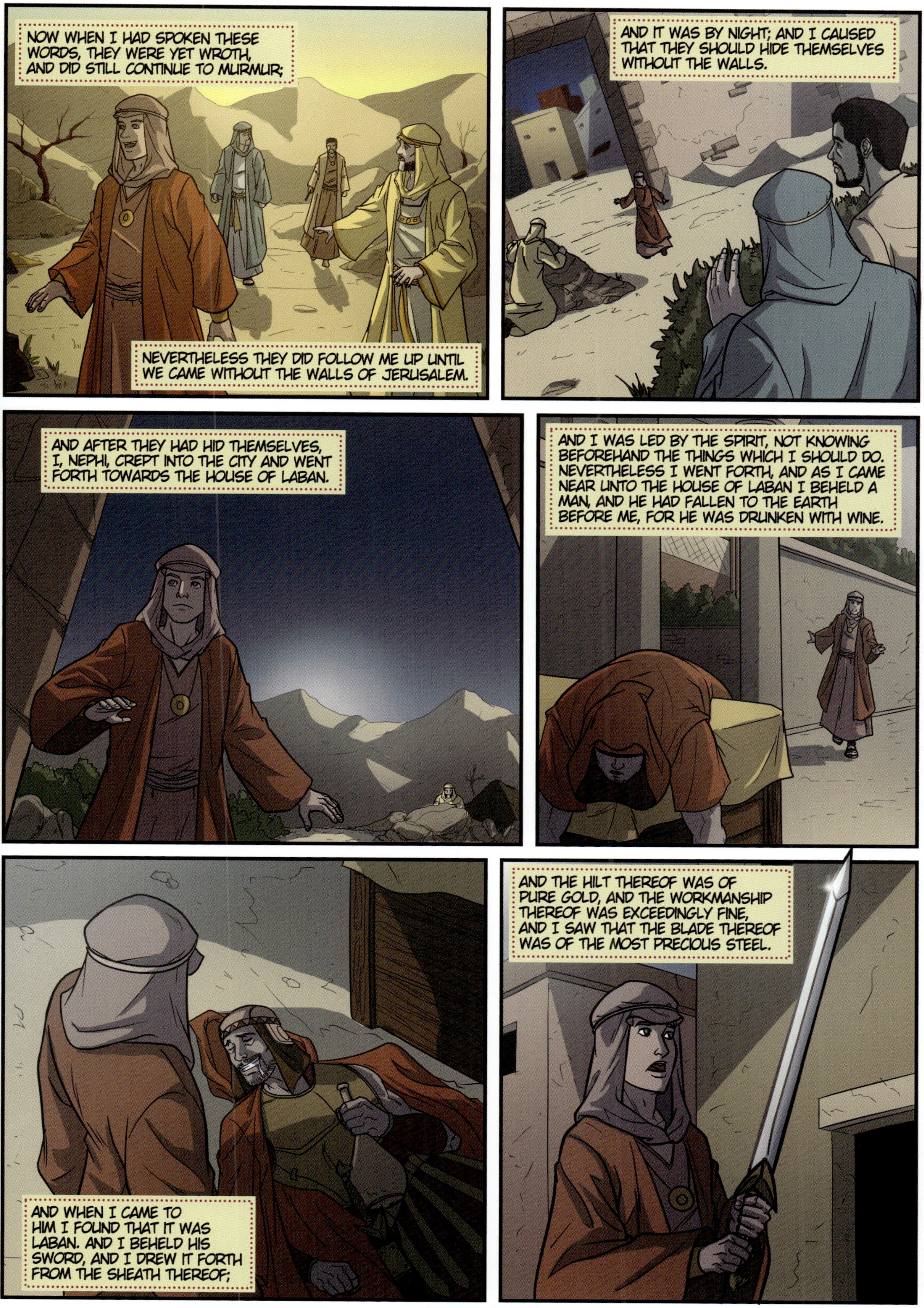
NOW WHEN I HAD SPOKEN THESE WORDS, THEY WERE YET WROTH, AND DID STILL CONTINUE TO MURMUR;
NEVERTHELESS THEY DID FOLLOW ME UP UNTIL WE CAME WITHOUT THE WALLS OF JERUSALEM.
AND IT WAS BY NIGHT; AND I CAUSED THAT THEY SHOULD HIDE THEMSELVES WITHOUT THE WALLS.
AND AFTER THEY HAD HID THEMSELVES, I, NEPHI, CREPT INTO THE CITY AND WENT FORTH TOWARDS THE HOUSE OF LABAN.
AND I WAS LED BY THE SPIRIT, NOT KNOWING BEFOREHAND THE THINGS WHICH I SHOULD DO. NEVERTHELESS I WENT FORTH, AND AS I CAME NEAR UNTO THE HOUSE OF LABAN I BEHELD A MAN, AND HE HAD FALLEN TO THE EARTH BEFORE ME, FOR HE WAS DRUNKEN WITH WINE.
AND WHEN I CAME TO HIM I FOUND THAT IT WAS LABAN. AND I BEHELD HIS SWORD, AND I DREW IT FORTH FROM THE SHEATH THEREOF;
AND THE HILT THEREOF WAS OF PURE GOLD, AND THE WORKMANSHIP THEREOF WAS EXCEEDINGLY FINE, AND I SAW THAT THE BLADE THEREOF WAS OF THE MOST PRECIOUS STEEL.

AND IT CAME TO PASS THAT I WAS CONSTRAINED BY THE SPIRIT THAT I SHOULD KILL LABAN; BUT I SAID IN MY HEART:
NEVER AT ANY TIME HAVE I SHED THE BLOOD OF MAN
AND I SHRUNK AND WOULD THAT I MIGHT NOT SLAY HIM. AND THE SPIRIT SAID UNTO ME AGAIN:
KILL LABAN, BEHOLD THE LORD HATH DELIVERED HIM INTO THY HANDS.
YEA, AND I ALSO KNEW THAT HE HAD SOUGHT TO TAKE AWAY MINE OWN LIFE;
YEA, AND HE WOULD NOT HEARKEN UNTO THE COMMANDMENTS OF THE LORD; AND HE ALSO HAD TAKEN AWAY OUR PROPERTY.
AND IT CAME TO PASS THAT THE SPIRIT SAID UNTO ME AGAIN:
SLAY HIM, FOR THE LORD HATH DELIVERED HIM INTO THY HANDS;
BEHOLD THE LORD SLAYETH THE WICKED TO BRING FORTH HIS RIGHTEOUS PURPOSES.
IT IS BETTER THAT ONE MAN SHOULD PERISH THAN THAT A NATION SHOULD DWINDLE AND PERISH IN UNBELIEF.
AND NOW, WHEN I, NEPHI, HAD HEARD THESE WORDS, I REMEMBERED THE WORDS OF THE LORD WHICH HE SPAKE UNTO ME IN THE WILDERNESS, SAYING THAT:
INASMUCH AS THY SEED SHALL KEEP MY COMMANDMENTS, THEY SHALL PROSPER IN THE LAND OF PROMISE.
YEA, AND I ALSO THOUGHT THAT THEY COULD NOT KEEP THE COMMANDMENTS OF THE LORD ACCORDING TO THE LAW OF MOSES, SAVE THEY SHOULD HAVE THE LAW. AND I ALSO KNEW THAT THE LAW WAS ENGRAVEN UPON THE PLATES OF BRASS.

AND AGAIN, I KNEW THAT THE LORD HAD DELIVERED LABAN INTO MY HANDS FOR THIS CAUSE...
THAT I MIGHT OBTAIN THE RECORDS ACCORDING TO HIS COMMANDMENTS.
THEREFORE I DID OBEY THE VOICE OF THE SPIRIT, AND TOOK LABAN BY THE HAIR OF THE HEAD, AND I SMOTE OFF HIS HEAD WITH HIS OWN SWORD.
AND AFTER I HAD SMITTEN OFF HIS HEAD WITH HIS OWN SWORD, I TOOK THE GARMENTS OF LABAN...
AND PUT THEM UPON MINE OWN BODY;
YEA, EVEN EVERY WHIT; AND I DID GIRD ON HIS ARMOR ABOUT MY LOINS.
AND AFTER I HAD DONE THIS, I WENT FORTH UNTO THE TREASURY OF LABAN. AND AS I WENT FORTH TOWARDS THE TREASURY OF LABAN, BEHOLD, I SAW THE SERVANT OF LABAN WHO HAD THE KEYS OF THE TREASURY.

AND I COMMANDED HIM IN THE VOICE OF LABAN, THAT HE SHOULD GO WITH ME INTO THE TREASURY.
GO WITH ME INTO THE TREASURY...
AND HE SUPPOSED ME TO BE HIS MASTER, LABAN, FOR HE BEHELD THE GARMENTS AND ALSO THE SWORD GIRDED ABOUT MY LOINS.
AND HE SPAKE UNTO ME CONCERNING THE ELDERS OF THE JEWS, HE KNOWING THAT HIS MASTER, LABAN, HAD BEEN OUT BY NIGHT AMONG THEM. AND I SPAKE UNTO HIM AS IF IT HAD BEEN LABAN.
AND I ALSO SPAKE UNTO HIM THAT I SHOULD CARRY THE ENGRAVINGS, WHICH WERE UPON THE PLATES OF BRASS, TO MY ELDER BRETHREN, WHO WERE WITHOUT THE WALLS.
AND I ALSO BADE HIM THAT HE SHOULD FOLLOW ME.
MASTER, WHAT OF THE ELDERS OF THE JEWS?
AND HE, SUPPOSING THAT I SPAKE OF THE BRETHREN OF THE CHURCH, AND THAT I WAS TRULY THAT LABAN WHOM I HAD SLAIN, WHEREFORE HE DID FOLLOW ME. AND HE SPAKE UNTO ME MANY TIMES CONCERNING THE ELDERS OF THE JEWS, AS I WENT FORTH UNTO MY BRETHREN, WHO WERE WITHOUT THE WALLS.

AND IT CAME TO PASS THAT WHEN LAMAN SAW ME HE WAS EXCEEDINGLY FRIGHTENED, AND ALSO LEMUEL AND SAM. AND THEY FLED FROM BEFORE MY PRESENCE; FOR THEY SUPPOSED IT WAS LABAN, AND THAT HE HAD SLAIN ME AND HAD SOUGHT TO TAKE AWAY THEIR LIVES ALSO.
AND IT CAME TO PASS THAT I CALLED AFTER THEM, AND THEY DID HEAR ME; WHEREFORE THEY DID CEASE TO FLEE FROM MY PRESENCE.
AND IT CAME TO PASS THAT WHEN THE SERVANT OF LABAN BEHELD MY BRETHREN HE BEGAN TO TREMBLE, AND WAS ABOUT TO FLEE FROM BEFORE ME AND RETURN TO THE CITY OF JERUSALEM. AND NOW I, NEPHI, BEING A MAN LARGE IN STATURE, AND ALSO HAVING RECEIVED MUCH STRENGTH OF THE LORD, THEREFORE I DID SEIZE UPON THE SERVANT OF LABAN......
AS THE LORD LIVETH, AND AS I LIVE, EVEN SO, IF YOU WILL HEARKEN UNTO OUR WORDS, WE WILL SPARE YOUR LIFE.
AND HELD HIM, THAT HE SHOULD NOT FLEE. AND IT CAME TO PASS THAT I SPAKE WITH HIM, THAT IF HE WOULD HEARKEN UNTO MY WORDS,, AS THE LORD LIVETH, AND AS I LIVE, EVEN SO THAT THAT IF HE SOULD HEARKEN UNTO OUR WORDS WE WOULD SPARE HIS LIFE...
AND I SPAKE UNTO HIM, EVEN WITH AN OATH, THAT HE NEED NOT FEAR;

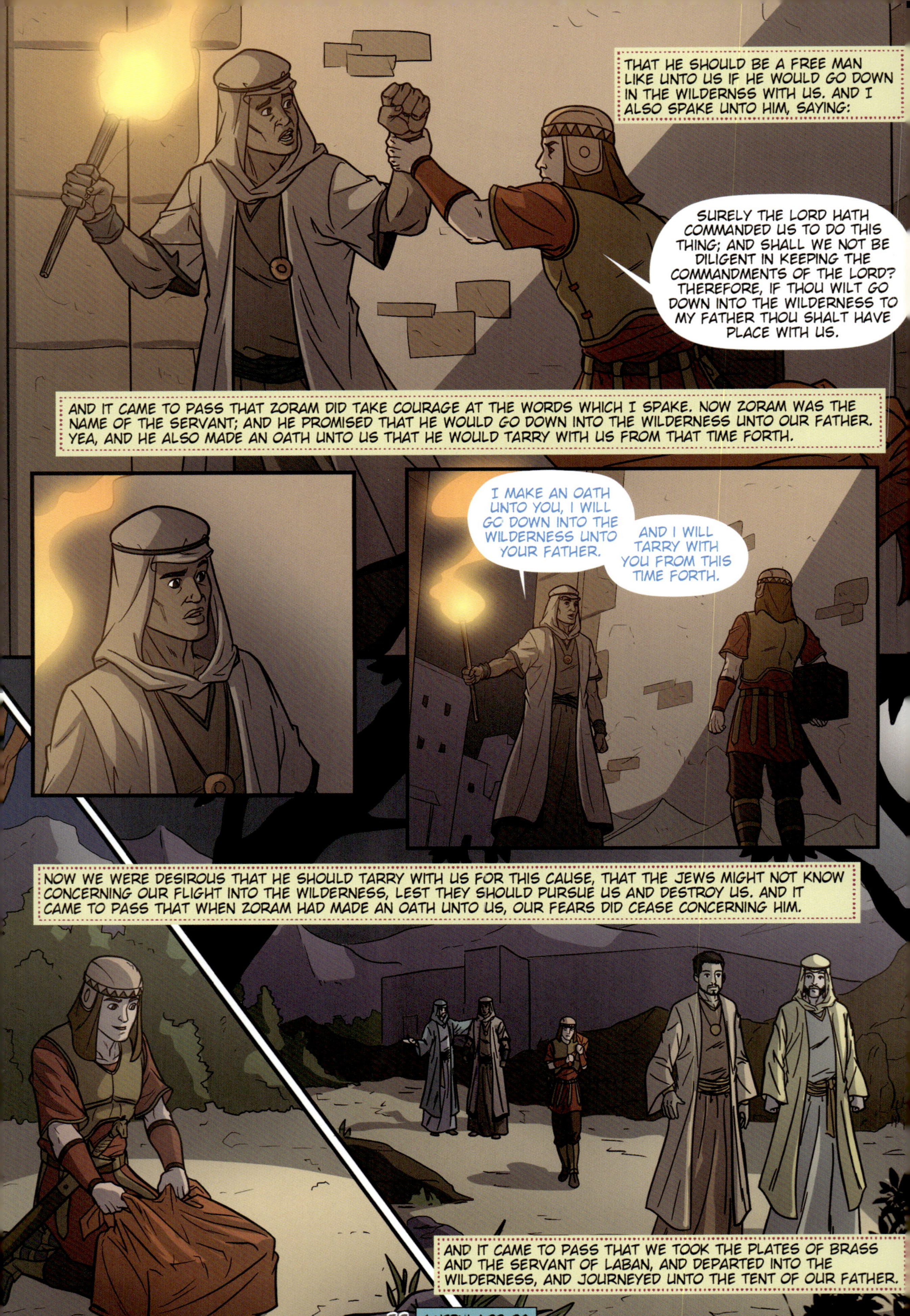
THAT HE SHOULD BE A FREE MAN LIKE UNTO US IF HE WOULD GO DOWN IN THE WILDERNSS WITH US. AND I ALSO SPAKE UNTO HIM, SAYING:
SURELY THE LORD HATH COMMANDED US TO DO THIS THING; AND SHALL WE NOT BE DILIGENT IN KEEPING THE COMMANDMENTS OF THE LORD? THEREFORE, IF THOU WILT GO DOWN INTO THE WILDERNESS TO MY FATHER THOU SHALT HAVE PLACE WITH US.
AND IT CAME TO PASS THAT ZORAM DID TAKE COURAGE AT THE WORDS WHICH I SPAKE. NOW ZORAM WAS THE NAME OF THE SERVANT; AND HE PROMISED THAT HE WOULD GO DOWN INTO THE WILDERNESS UNTO OUR FATHER. YEA, AND HE ALSO MADE AN OATH UNTO US THAT HE WOULD TARRY WITH US FROM THAT TIME FORTH.
I MAKE AN OATH UNTO YOU, I WILL GO DOWN INTO THE WILDERNESS UNTO YOUR FATHER.
AND I WILL TARRY WITH YOU FROM THIS TIME FORTH.
NOW WE WERE DESIROUS THAT HE SHOULD TARRY WITH US FOR THIS CAUSE, THAT THE JEWS MIGHT NOT KNOW CONCERNING OUR FLIGHT INTO THE WILDERNESS, LEST THEY SHOULD PURSUE US AND DESTROY US. AND IT CAME TO PASS THAT WHEN ZORAM HAD MADE AN OATH UNTO US, OUR FEARS DID CEASE CONCERNING HIM.
AND IT CAME TO PASS THAT WE TOOK THE PLATES OF BRASS AND THE SERVANT OF LABAN, AND DEPARTED INTO THE WILDERNESS, AND JOURNEYED UNTO THE TENT OF OUR FATHER.

COVER VARIANT FOR ISSUE 1
BASED ON CHAPTER 2:
LEHI DEPARTS WITH HIS FAMILY

COVER VARIANT FOR ISSUE 1
BASED ON CHAPTER 4:
NEPHI OBTAINS THE PLATES FROM ZORAM

AND IT CAME TO PASS THAT AFTER WE HAD COME DOWN INTO THE WILDERNESS UNTO OUR FATHER, BEHOLD, HE WAS FILLED WITH JOY,
AND ALSO MY MOTHER, SARIAH, WAS EXCEEDINGLY GLAD,
FOR SHE TRULY HAD MOURNED BECAUSE OF US.
FOR SHE HAD SUPPOSED THAT WE HAD PERISHED...
IN THE WILDERNESS;

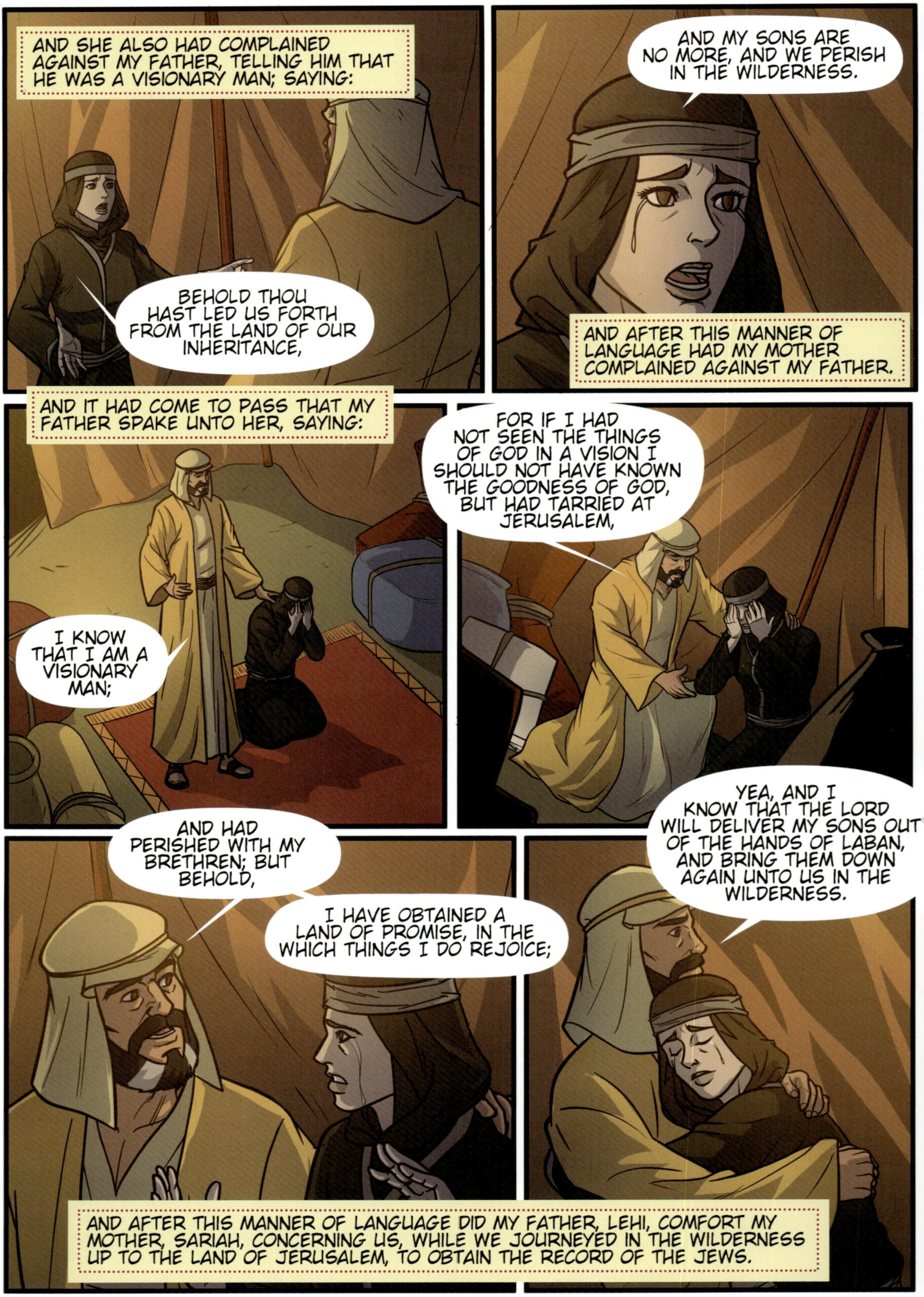
AND SHE ALSO HAD COMPLAINED AGAINST MY FATHER, TELLING HIM THAT HE WAS A VISIONARY MAN; SAYING:
BEHOLD THOU HAST LED US FORTH FROM THE LAND OF OUR INHERITANCE,
AND MY SONS ARE NO MORE, AND WE PERISH IN THE WILDERNESS.
AND AFTER THIS MANNER OF LANGUAGE HAD MY MOTHER COMPLAINED AGAINST MY FATHER.
AND IT HAD COME TO PASS THAT MY FATHER SPAKE UNTO HER, SAYING:
I KNOW THAT I AM A VISIONARY MAN;
FOR IF I HAD NOT SEEN THE THINGS OF GOD IN A VISION I SHOULD NOT HAVE KNOWN THE GOODNESS OF GOD, BUT HAD TARRIED AT JERUSALEM,
AND HAD PERISHED WITH MY BRETHREN; BUT BEHOLD,
I HAVE OBTAINED A LAND OF PROMISE, IN THE WHICH THINGS I DO REJOICE;
YEA, AND I KNOW THAT THE LORD WILL DELIVER MY SONS OUT OF THE HANDS OF LABAN, AND BRING THEM DOWN AGAIN UNTO US IN THE WILDERNESS.
AND AFTER THIS MANNER OF LANGUAGE DID MY FATHER, LEHI, COMFORT MY MOTHER, SARIAH, CONCERNING US, WHILE WE JOURNEYED IN THE WILDERNESS UP TO THE LAND OF JERUSALEM, TO OBTAIN THE RECORD OF THE JEWS.

AND WHEN WE HAD RETURNED TO THE TENT OF MY FATHER,
BEHOLD THEIR JOY WAS FULL, AND MY MOTHER WAS COMFORTED. AND SHE SPAKE, SAYING:
NOW I KNOW OF A SURETY THAT THE LORD HATH COMMANDED MY HUSBAND TO FLEE INTO THE WILDERNESS;
YEA, AND I ALSO KNOW OF A SURETY THAT THE LORD HATH PROTECTED MY SONS,
AND DELIVERED THEM OUT OF THE HANDS OF LABAN,
AND GIVEN THEM POWER WHEREBY THEY COULD ACCOMPLISH THE THING WHICH THE LORD HATH COMMANDED THEM.
AND AFTER THIS MANNER OF LANGUAGE DID SHE SPEAK. AND IT CAME TO PASS THAT THEY DID REJOICE EXCEEDINGLY, AND DID OFFER SACRIFICE AND BURNT OFFERINGS UNTO THE LORD; AND THEY GAVE THANKS UNTO THE GOD OF ISRAEL.

AND AFTER THEY HAD GIVEN THANKS UNTO THE GOD OF ISRAEL, MY FATHER, LEHI, TOOK THE RECORDS WHICH WERE ENGRAVEN UPON THE PLATES OF BRASS,
AND HE DID SEARCH THEM FROM THE BEGINNING.
AND HE BEHELD THAT THEY DID CONTAIN THE FIVE BOOKS OF MOSES, WHICH GAVE AN ACCOUNT OF THE CREATION OF THE WORLD, AND ALSO OF ADAM AND EVE, WHO WERE OUR FIRST PARENTS;
AND ALSO A RECORD OF THE JEWS FROM THE BEGINNING, EVEN DOWN TO THE COMMENCEMENT OF THE REIGN OF ZEDEKIAH, KING OF JUDAH;
AND ALSO THE PROPHECIES OF THE HOLY PROPHETS, FROM THE BEGINNING, EVEN DOWN TO THE COMMENCEMENT OF THE REIGN OF ZEDEKIAH;
AND ALSO MANY PROPHECIES WHICH HAVE BEEN SPOKEN BY THE MOUTH OF JEREMIAH.

AND IT CAME TO PASS THAT MY FATHER, LEHI, ALSO FOUND UPON THE PLATES OF BRASS A GENEALOGY OF HIS FATHERS; WHEREFORE HE KNEW THAT HE WAS A DESCENDANT OF JOSEPH;
YEA, EVEN THAT JOSEPH WHO WAS THE SON OF JACOB, WHO WAS SOLD INTO EGYPT, AND WHO WAS PRESERVED BY THE HAND OF THE LORD,
THAT HE MIGHT PRESERVE HIS FATHER, JACOB, AND ALL HIS HOUSEHOLD FROM PERISHING WITH FAMINE.
AND THEY WERE ALSO LED OUT OF CAPTIVITY AND OUT OF THE LAND OF EGYPT, BY THAT SAME GOD WHO HAD PRESERVED THEM.
AND THUS MY FATHER, LEHI, DID DISCOVER THE GENEALOGY OF HIS FATHERS. AND LABAN ALSO WAS A DESCENDANT OF JOSEPH, WHEREFORE HE AND HIS FATHERS HAD KEPT THE RECORDS.

AND NOW WHEN MY FATHER SAW ALL THESE THINGS, HE WAS FILLED WITH THE SPIRIT, AND BEGAN TO PROPHESY CONCERNING HIS SEED--
THAT THESE PLATES OF BRASS SHOULD GO FORTH UNTO ALL NATIONS, KINDREDS, TONGUES, AND PEOPLE
WHO WERE OF HIS SEED.
WHEREFORE, HE SAID THAT
THESE PLATES OF BRASS SHOULD NEVER PERISH; NEITHER SHOULD THEY BE DIMMED ANY MORE BY TIME.
AND HE PROPHESIED MANY THINGS CONCERNING HIS SEED.
AND IT CAME TO PASS THAT THUS FAR I AND MY FATHER HAD KEPT THE COMMANDMENTS WHEREWITH THE LORD HAD COMMANDED US. AND WE HAD OBTAINED THE RECORDS WHICH THE LORD HAD COMMANDED US, AND SEARCHED THEM AND FOUND THAT THEY WERE DESIRABLE;
YEA, EVEN OF GREAT WORTH UNTO US, INSOMUCH THAT WE COULD PRESERVE THE COMMANDMENTS OF THE LORD UNTO OUR CHILDREN. WHEREFORE, IT WAS WISDOM IN THE LORD THAT WE SHOULD CARRY THEM WITH US, AS WE JOURNEYED IN THE WILDERNESS TOWARDS THE LAND OF PROMISE.

AND NOW I, NEPHI, DO NOT GIVE THE GENEALOGY OF MY FATHERS IN THIS PART OF MY RECORD; NEITHER AT ANY TIME SHALL I GIVE IT AFTER UPON THESE PLATES WHICH I AM WRITING; FOR IT IS GIVEN IN THE RECORD WHICH HAS BEEN KEPT BY MY FATHER; WHEREFORE, I DO NOT WRITE IT IN THIS WORK.
FOR IT SUFFICETH ME TO SAY THAT WE ARE DESCENDANTS OF JOSEPH.
AND IT MATTERETH NOT TO ME THAT I AM PARTICULAR TO GIVE A FULL ACCOUNT OF ALL THE THINGS OF MY FATHER, FOR THEY CANNOT BE WRITTEN UPON THESE PLATES, FOR I DESIRE THE ROOM THAT I MAY WRITE OF THE THINGS OF GOD.
FOR THE FULNESS OF MINE INTENT IS THAT I MAY PERSUADE MEN TO COME UNTO THE GOD OF ABRAHAM, AND THE GOD OF ISAAC, AND THE GOD OF JACOB,
AND BE SAVED.
WHEREFORE, THE THINGS WHICH ARE PLEASING UNTO THE WORLD I DO NOT WRITE, BUT THE THINGS WHICH ARE PLEASING UNTO GOD AND UNTO THOSE WHO ARE NOT OF THE WORLD. WHEREFORE, I SHALL GIVE COMMANDMENT UNTO MY SEED, THAT THEY SHALL NOT OCCUPY THESE PLATES WITH THINGS WHICH ARE NOT OF WORTH UNTO THE CHILDREN OF MEN.

AND NOW I WOULD THAT YE MIGHT KNOW, THAT AFTER MY FATHER, LEHI, HAD MADE AN END OF PROPHESYING CONCERNING HIS SEED,
IT CAME TO PASS THAT THE LORD SPAKE UNTO HIM AGAIN,
SAYING THAT IT WAS NOT MEET FOR HIM, LEHI, THAT HE SHOULD TAKE HIS FAMILY INTO THE WILDERNESS ALONE;
BUT THAT HIS SONS SHOULD TAKE DAUGHTERS TO WIFE, THAT THEY MIGHT RAISE UP SEED UNTO THE LORD IN THE LAND OF PROMISE.
IT IS NOT MEET FOR YOU, LEHI, THAT YOU SHOULD TAKE YOUR FAMILY INTO THE WILDERNESS ALONE;
BUT YOUR SONS SHOULD TAKE DAUGHTERS TO WIFE, THAT THEY MIGHT RAISE UP SEED UNTO ME IN THE LAND OF PROMISE.
AND IT CAME TO PASS THAT THE LORD COMMANDED HIM THAT I, NEPHI, AND MY BRETHREN, SHOULD AGAIN RETURN UNTO THE LAND OF JERUSALEM,...
NEPHI, AND HIS BRETHREN, SHALL AGAIN RETURN UNTO THE LAND OF JERUSALEM, AND BRING DOWN ISHMAEL AND HIS FAMILY INTO THE WILDERNESS.

AND IT CAME TO PASS THAT I, NEPHI, DID AGAIN, WITH MY BRETHREN, GO FORTH INTO THE WILDERNESS TO GO UP TO JERUSALEM.
AND IT CAME TO PASS THAT WE WENT UP UNTO THE HOUSE OF ISHMAEL,
AND WE DID GAIN FAVOR IN THE SIGHT OF ISHMAEL
INSOMUCH THAT WE DID SPEAK UNTO HIM THE WORDS OF THE LORD.

AND IT CAME TO PASS THAT THE LORD DID SOFTEN THE HEART OF ISHMAEL,
AND ALSO HIS HOUSEHOLD,
INSOMUCH THAT THEY TOOK THEIR JOURNEY WITH US DOWN INTO THE WILDERNESS TO THE TENT OF OUR FATHER.

AND IT CAME TO PASS THAT AS WE JOURNEYED IN THE WILDERNESS, BEHOLD LAMAN AND LEMUEL, AND TWO OF THE DAUGHTERS OF ISHMAEL, AND THE TWO SONS OF ISHMAEL AND THEIR FAMILIES, DID REBEL AGAINST US;
YEA, AGAINST ME, NEPHI, AND SAM, AND THEIR FATHER, ISHMAEL, AND HIS WIFE, AND HIS THREE OTHER DAUGHTERS. AND IT CAME TO PASS IN THE WHICH REBELLION, THEY WERE DESIROUS TO RETURN UNTO THE LAND OF JERUSALEM.
AND NOW I, NEPHI, BEING GRIEVED FOR THE HARDNESS OF THEIR HEARTS, THEREFORE I SPAKE UNTO THEM, SAYING, YEA, EVEN UNTO LAMAN AND UNTO LEMUEL:
BEHOLD YE ARE MINE ELDER BRETHREN, AND HOW IS IT THAT YE ARE SO HARD IN YOUR HEARTS, AND SO BLIND IN YOUR MINDS,
THAT YE HAVE NEED THAT I, YOUR YOUNGER BROTHER, SHOULD SPEAK UNTO YOU,
YEA, AND SET AN EXAMPLE FOR YOU?
HOW IS IT THAT YE HAVE NOT HEARKENED UNTO THE WORD OF THE LORD?
HOW IS IT THAT YE HAVE FORGOTTEN THAT YE HAVE SEEN AN ANGEL OF THE LORD?
YEA, AND HOW IS IT THAT YE HAVE FORGOTTEN WHAT GREAT THINGS THE LORD HATH DONE FOR US, IN DELIVERING US OUT OF THE HANDS OF LABAN, AND ALSO THAT WE SHOULD OBTAIN THE RECORD?

YEA, AND HOW IS IT THAT YE HAVE FORGOTTEN THAT THE LORD IS ABLE TO DO ALL THINGS ACCORDING TO HIS WILL, FOR THE CHILDREN OF MEN,
IF IT SO BE THAT THEY EXERCISE FAITH IN HIM. . .
WHEREFORE, LET US BE FAITHFUL TO HIM.
AND IF IT SO BE THAT WE ARE FAITHFUL TO HIM, WE SHALL OBTAIN THE LAND OF PROMISE;
AND YE SHALL KNOW AT SOME FUTURE PERIOD THAT THE WORD OF THE LORD SHALL BE FULFILLED CONCERNING THE DESTRUCTION OF JERUSALEM;
FOR ALL THINGS WHICH THE LORD HATH SPOKEN CONCERNING THE DESTRUCTION OF JERUSALEM MUST BE FULFILLED.
FOR BEHOLD, THE SPIRIT OF THE LORD CEASETH SOON TO STRIVE WITH THEM;
FOR BEHOLD, THEY HAVE REJECTED THE PROPHETS,
AND JEREMIAH HAVE THEY CAST INTO PRISON.

AND THEY HAVE SOUGHT TO TAKE AWAY THE LIFE OF MY FATHER, INSOMUCH THAT THEY HAVE DRIVEN HIM OUT OF THE LAND.
NOW BEHOLD, I SAY UNTO YOU THAT IF YE WILL RETURN UNTO JERUSALEM YE SHALL ALSO PERISH WITH THEM.
AND NOW, IF YE HAVE CHOICE, GO UP TO THE LAND, AND REMEMBER THE WORDS WHICH I SPEAK UNTO YOU,
THAT IF YE GO YE WILL ALSO PERISH;
FOR THUS THE SPIRIT OF THE LORD CONSTRAINETH ME THAT I SHOULD SPEAK.
AND IT CAME TO PASS THAT WHEN I, NEPHI, HAD SPOKEN THESE WORDS UNTO MY BRETHREN, THEY WERE ANGRY WITH ME.
AND IT CAME TO PASS THAT THEY DID LAY THEIR HANDS UPON ME, FOR BEHOLD, THEY WERE EXCEEDINGLY WROTH,
AND THEY DID BIND ME WITH CORDS, FOR THEY SOUGHT TO TAKE AWAY MY LIFE, THAT THEY MIGHT LEAVE ME IN THE WILDERNESS
TO BE DEVOURED BY WILD BEASTS.

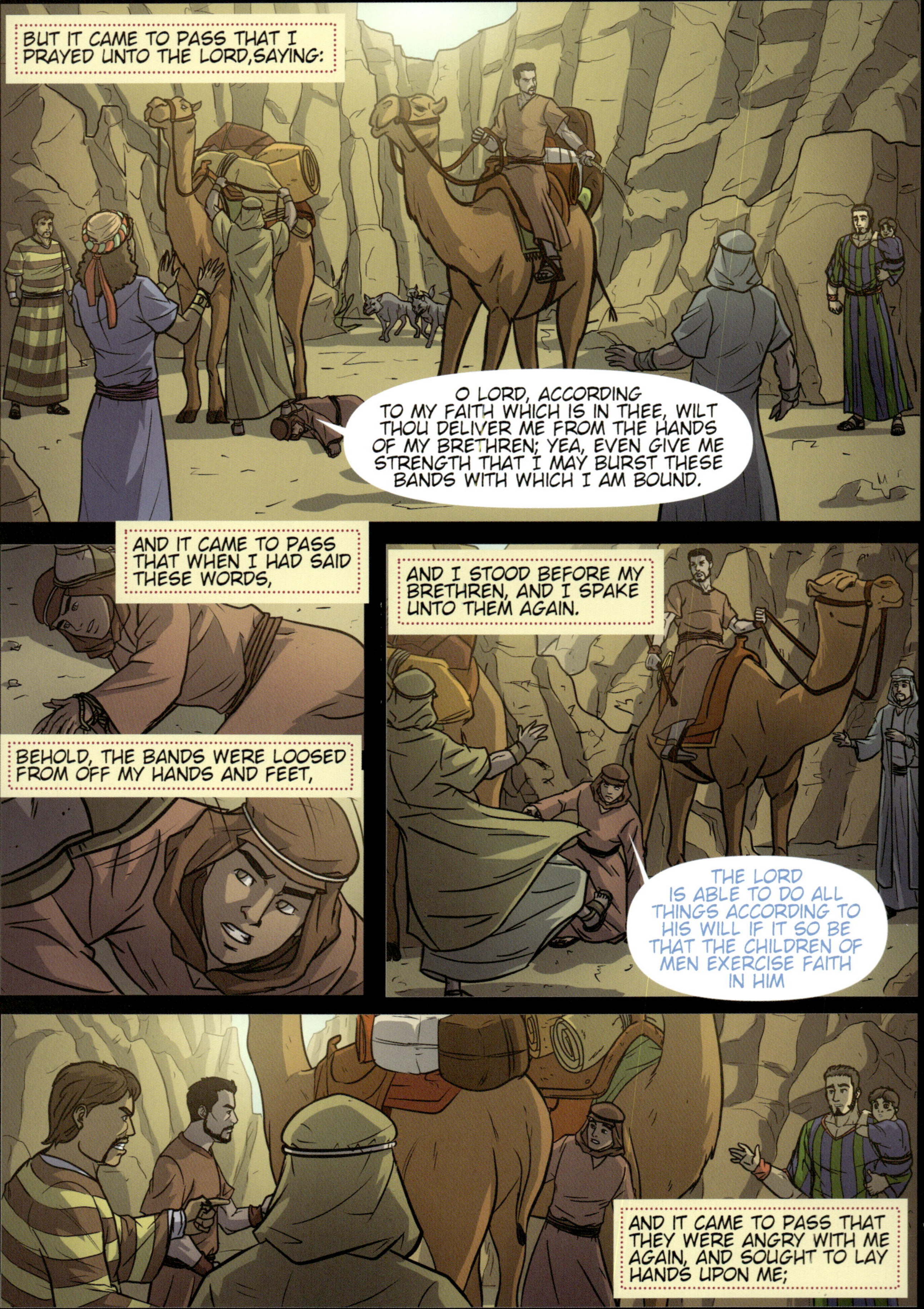
BUT IT CAME TO PASS THAT I PRAYED UNTO THE LORD, SAYING:
O LORD, ACCORDING TO MY FAITH WHICH IS IN THEE, WILT THOU DELIVER ME FROM THE HANDS OF MY BRETHREN; YEA, EVEN GIVE ME STRENGTH THAT I MAY BURST THESE BANDS WITH WHICH I AM BOUND.
AND IT CAME TO PASS THAT WHEN I HAD SAID THESE WORDS,
BEHOLD, THE BANDS WERE LOOSED FROM OFF MY HANDS AND FEET,
AND I STOOD BEFORE MY BRETHREN, AND I SPAKE UNTO THEM AGAIN.
THE LORD IS ABLE TO DO ALL THINGS ACCORDING TO HIS WILL IF IT SO BE THAT THE CHILDREN OF MEN EXERCISE FAITH IN HIM
AND IT CAME TO PASS THAT THEY WERE ANGRY WITH ME AGAIN, AND SOUGHT TO LAY HANDS UPON ME;

BUT BEHOLD, ONE OF THE DAUGHTERS OF ISHMAEL, YEA, AND ALSO HER MOTHER, AND ONE OF THE SONS OF ISHMAEL, DID PLEAD WITH MY BRETHREN,
INSOMUCH THAT THEY DID SOFTEN THEIR HEARTS; AND THEY DID CEASE STRIVING TO TAKE AWAY MY LIFE.
AND IT CAME TO PASS THAT THEY WERE SORROWFUL, BECAUSE OF THEIR WICKEDNESS, INSOMUCH THAT THEY DID BOW DOWN BEFORE ME, AND DID PLEAD WITH ME THAT I WOULD FORGIVE THEM OF THE THING THAT THEY HAD DONE AGAINST ME.

I FORGIVE YOU.
AND IT CAME TO PASS THAT I DID FRANKLY FORGIVE THEM ALL THAT THEY HAD DONE,
AND I DID EXHORT THEM THAT THEY WOULD PRAY UNTO THE LORD THEIR GOD FOR FORGIVENESS.
PRAY UNTO THE LORD OUR GOD FOR FORGIVENESS.
AND IT CAME TO PASS THAT THEY DID SO.
AND AFTER THEY HAD DONE PRAYING UNTO THE LORD WE DID AGAIN TRAVEL ON OUR JOURNEY TOWARDS THE TENT OF OUR FATHER.
AND IT CAME TO PASS THAT WE DID COME DOWN UNTO THE TENT OF OUR FATHER.

AND AFTER I AND MY BRETHREN AND ALL THE HOUSE OF ISHMAEL HAD COME DOWN UNTO THE TENT OF MY FATHER, THEY DID GIVE THANKS UNTO THE LORD THEIR GOD;
AND THEY DID OFFER SACRIFICE AND BURNT OFFERINGS UNTO HIM.
AND IT CAME TO PASS THAT WE HAD GATHERED TOGETHER ALL MANNER OF SEEDS OF EVERY KIND, BOTH OF GRAIN OF EVERY KIND, AND ALSO OF THE SEEDS OF FRUIT OF EVERY KIND.
AND IT CAME TO PASS THAT WHILE MY FATHER TARRIED IN THE WILDERNESS HE SPAKE UNTO US, SAYING:
BEHOLD, I HAVE DREAMED A DREAM; OR, IN OTHER WORDS, I HAVE SEEN A VISION.

AND BEHOLD, BECAUSE OF THE THING WHICH I HAVE SEEN, I HAVE REASON TO REJOICE IN THE LORD BECAUSE OF NEPHI AND ALSO OF SAM;
FOR I HAVE REASON TO SUPPOSE THAT THEY, AND ALSO MANY OF THEIR SEED, WILL BE SAVED.
BUT BEHOLD, LAMAN AND LEMUEL, I FEAR EXCEEDINGLY BECAUSE OF YOU;
FOR BEHOLD, METHOUGHT I SAW IN MY DREAM, A DARK AND DREARY WILDERNESS. AND IT CAME TO PASS THAT I SAW A MAN, AND HE WAS DRESSED IN A WHITE ROBE;

AND HE CAME AND STOOD BEFORE ME. AND IT CAME TO PASS THAT HE SPAKE UNTO ME, AND BADE ME FOLLOW HIM.
FOLLOW ME.
AND IT CAME TO PASS THAT AS I FOLLOWED HIM I BEHELD MYSELF THAT I WAS IN A DARK AND DREARY WASTE.
AND AFTER I HAD TRAVELED FOR THE SPACE OF MANY HOURS IN DARKNESS, I BEGAN TO PRAY UNTO THE LORD THAT HE WOULD HAVE MERCY ON ME, ACCORDING TO THE MULTITUDE OF HIS TENDER MERCIES.
LORD, HAVE MERCY ON ME.
AND IT CAME TO PASS AFTER I HAD PRAYED UNTO THE LORD I BEHELD A LARGE AND SPACIOUS FIELD. AND IT CAME TO PASS THAT I BEHELD A TREE, WHOSE FRUIT WAS DESIRABLE TO MAKE ONE HAPPY.

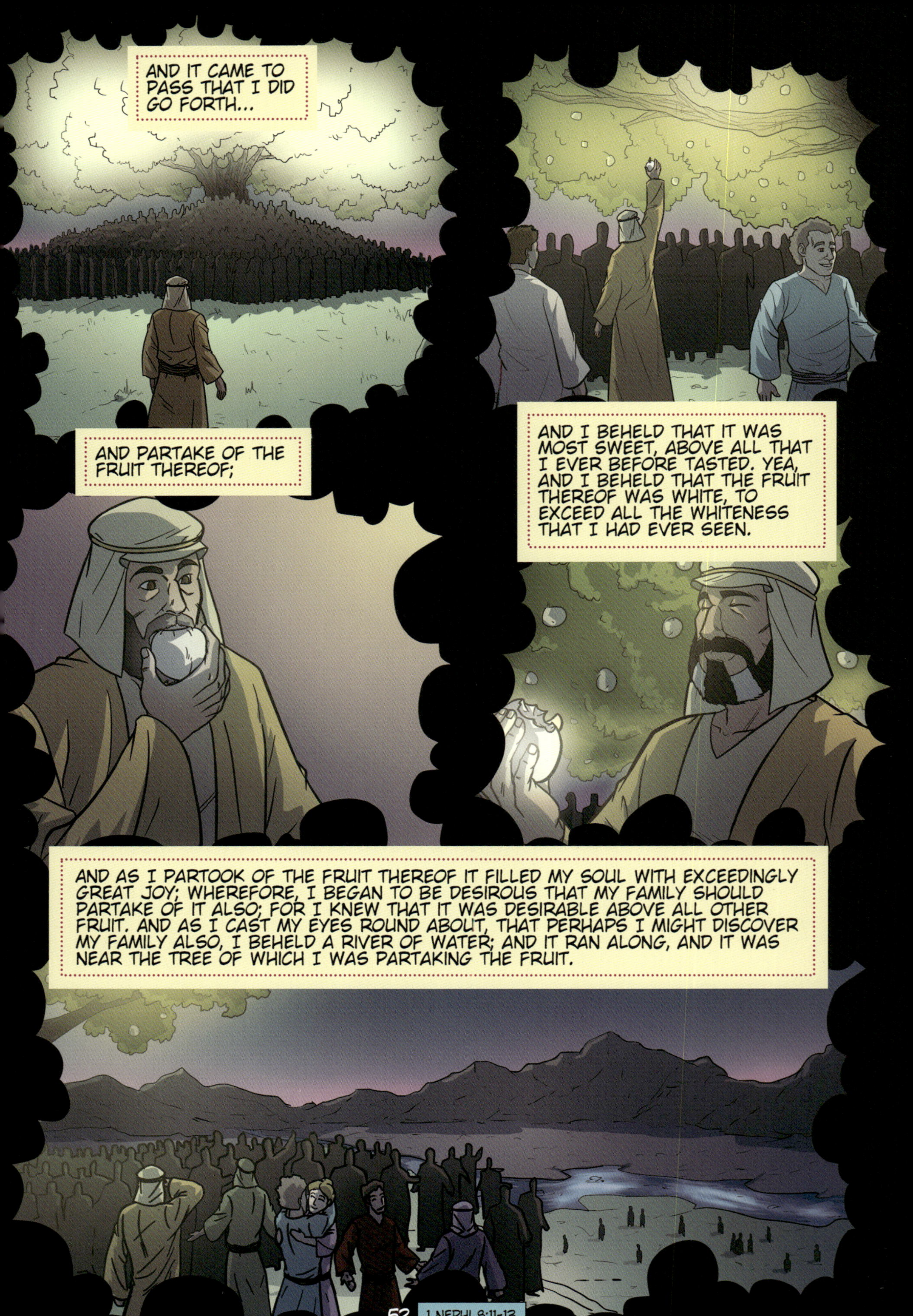
AND IT CAME TO PASS THAT I DID GO FORTH...
AND PARTAKE OF THE FRUIT THEREOF;
AND I BEHELD THAT IT WAS MOST SWEET, ABOVE ALL THAT I EVER BEFORE TASTED. YEA, AND I BEHELD THAT THE FRUIT THEREOF WAS WHITE, TO EXCEED ALL THE WHITENESS THAT I HAD EVER SEEN.
AND AS I PARTOOK OF THE FRUIT THEREOF IT FILLED MY SOUL WITH EXCEEDINGLY GREAT JOY; WHEREFORE, I BEGAN TO BE DESIROUS THAT MY FAMILY SHOULD PARTAKE OF IT ALSO; FOR I KNEW THAT IT WAS DESIRABLE ABOVE ALL OTHER FRUIT. AND AS I CAST MY EYES ROUND ABOUT, THAT PERHAPS I MIGHT DISCOVER MY FAMILY ALSO, I BEHELD A RIVER OF WATER; AND IT RAN ALONG, AND IT WAS NEAR THE TREE OF WHICH I WAS PARTAKING THE FRUIT.

AND I LOOKED TO BEHOLD FROM WHENCE IT CAME; AND I SAW THE HEAD THEREOF A LITTLE WAY OFF; AND AT THE HEAD THEREOF I BEHELD YOUR MOTHER SARIAH, AND SAM, AND NEPHI; AND THEY STOOD AS IF THEY KNEW NOT WHITHER THEY SHOULD GO.
AND IT CAME TO PASS THAT I BECKONED UNTO THEM;
AND I ALSO DID SAY UNTO THEM WITH A LOUD VOICE THAT THEY SHOULD
COME UNTO ME, AND PARTAKE OF THE FRUIT,
WHICH WAS DESIRABLE ABOVE ALL OTHER FRUIT.
AND IT CAME TO PASS THAT THEY DID COME UNTO ME
AND PARTAKE OF THE FRUIT ALSO. AND IT CAME TO PASS THAT I WAS DESIROUS THAT LAMAN AND LEMUEL SHOULD COME AND PARTAKE OF THE FRUIT ALSO;

WHEREFORE, I CAST MINE EYES TOWARDS THE HEAD OF THE RIVER, THAT PERHAPS I MIGHT SEE THEM.
AND IT CAME TO PASS THAT I SAW THEM,
BUT THEY WOULD NOT COME UNTO ME AND PARTAKE OF THE FRUIT.
AND I BEHELD A ROD OF IRON, AND IT EXTENDED ALONG THE BANK OF THE RIVER, AND LED TO THE TREE BY WHICH I STOOD. AND I ALSO BEHELD A STRAIT AND NARROW PATH, WHICH CAME ALONG BY THE ROD OF IRON, EVEN TO THE TREE BY WHICH I STOOD; AND IT ALSO LED BY THE HEAD OF THE FOUNTAIN, UNTO A LARGE AND SPACIOUS FIELD, AS IF IT HAD BEEN A WORLD.

AND I SAW NUMBERLESS CONCOURSES OF PEOPLE, MANY OF WHOM WERE PRESSING FORWARD, THAT THEY MIGHT OBTAIN THE PATH WHICH LED UNTO THE TREE BY WHICH I STOOD.
AND IT CAME TO PASS THAT THEY DID COME FORTH, AND COMMENCE IN THE PATH WHICH LED TO THE TREE.
AND IT CAME TO PASS THAT THERE AROSE A MIST OF DARKNESS; YEA, EVEN AN EXCEEDINGLY GREAT MIST OF DARKNESS,
INSOMUCH THAT THEY WHO HAD COMMENCED IN THE PATH DID LOSE THEIR WAY, THAT THEY WANDERED OFF AND WERE LOST.

AND IT CAME TO PASS THAT I BEHELD OTHERS PRESSING FORWARD, AND THEY CAME FORTH AND CAUGHT HOLD OF THE END OF THE ROD OF IRON;
AND THEY DID PRESS FORWARD THROUGH THE MIST OF DARKNESS, CLINGING TO THE ROD OF IRON,
EVEN UNTIL THEY DID COME FORTH AND PARTAKE OF THE FRUIT OF THE TREE.
AND AFTER THEY HAD PARTAKEN OF THE FRUIT OF THE TREE THEY DID CAST THEIR EYES ABOUT AS IF THEY WERE ASHAMED.

AND I ALSO CAST MY EYES ROUND ABOUT,
AND BEHELD, ON THE OTHER SIDE OF THE RIVER OF WATER, A GREAT AND SPACIOUS BUILDING; AND IT STOOD AS IT WERE IN THE AIR, HIGH ABOVE THE EARTH.
AND IT WAS FILLED WITH PEOPLE, BOTH OLD AND YOUNG, BOTH MALE AND FEMALE; AND THEIR MANNER OF DRESS WAS EXCEEDINGLY FINE; AND THEY WERE IN THE ATTITUDE OF MOCKING AND POINTING THEIR FINGERS TOWARDS THOSE WHO HAD COME AT AND WERE PARTAKING OF THE FRUIT.
AND AFTER THEY HAD TASTED OF THE FRUIT THEY WERE ASHAMED, BECAUSE OF THOSE THAT WERE SCOFFING AT THEM; AND THEY FELL AWAY INTO FORBIDDEN PATHS AND WERE LOST.

AND NOW I, NEPHI, DO NOT SPEAK ALL THE WORDS OF MY FATHER. BUT TO BE SHORT IN WRITING, BEHOLD, HE SAW
...OTHER MULTITUDES PRESSING FORWARD; AND THEY CAME AND CAUGHT HOLD OF THE END OF THE ROD OF IRON; AND THEY DID PRESS THEIR WAY FORWARD,
CONTINUALLY HOLDING FAST TO THE ROD OF IRON,
UNTIL THEY CAME FORTH AND FELL DOWN AND PARTOOK OF THE FRUIT OF THE TREE.
AND HE ALSO SAW OTHER MULTITUDES FEELING THEIR WAY TOWARDS THAT GREAT AND SPACIOUS BUILDING.
AND IT CAME TO PASS THAT MANY WERE DROWNED IN THE DEPTHS OF THE FOUNTAIN;
AND MANY WERE LOST FROM HIS VIEW, WANDERING IN STRANGE ROADS.

AND GREAT WAS THE MULTITUDE THAT DID ENTER INTO THAT STRANGE BUILDING.
AND AFTER THEY DID ENTER INTO THAT BUILDING THEY DID POINT THE FINGER OF SCORN AT ME AND THOSE THAT WERE PARTAKING OF THE FRUIT ALSO;
BUT WE HEEDED THEM NOT.
THESE WERE THE WORDS OF MY FATHER: FOR AS MANY AS HEEDED THEM, HAD FALLEN AWAY.
AND LAMAN AND LEMUEL PARTOOK NOT OF THE FRUIT, SAID MY FATHER.

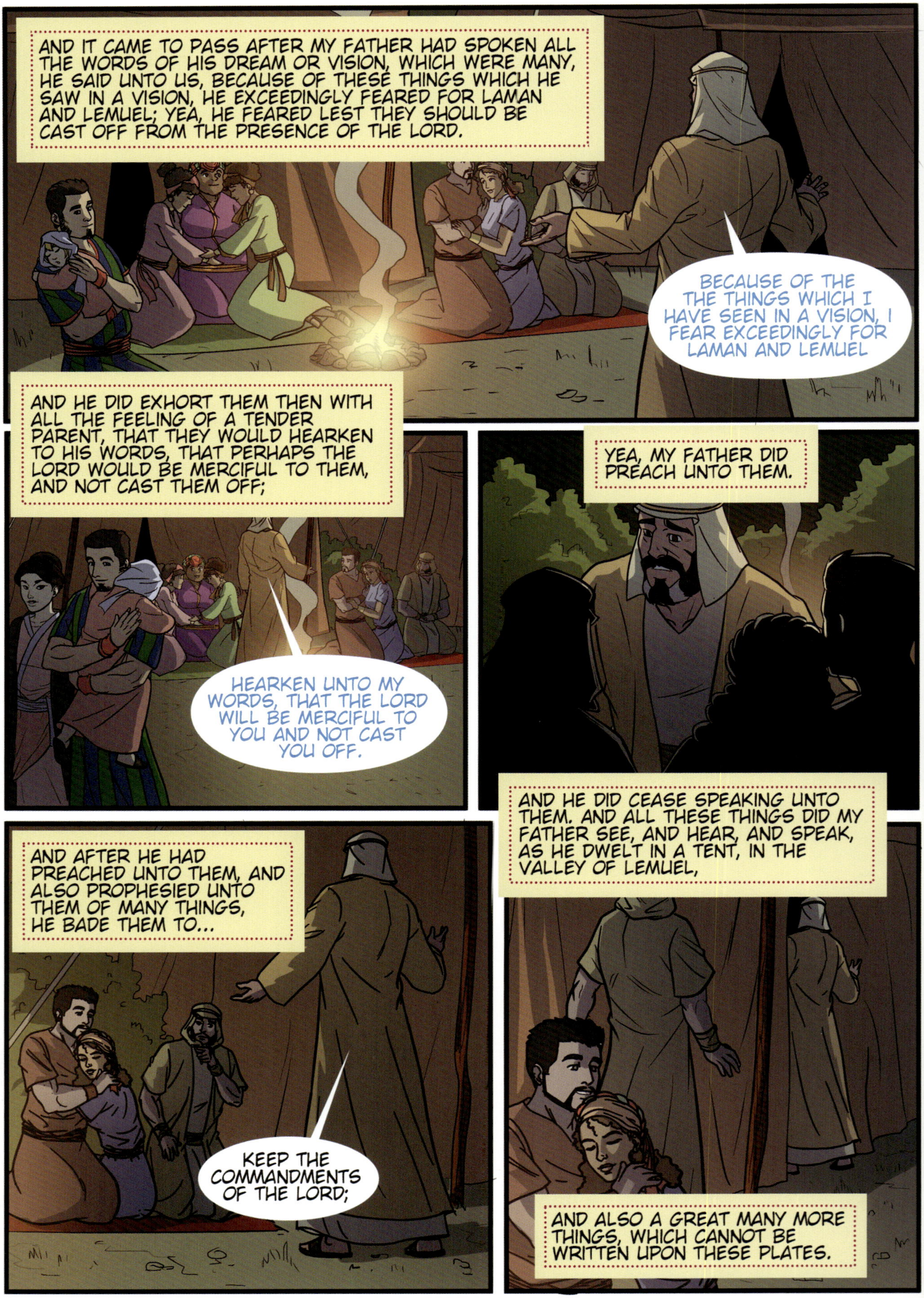

AND IT CAME TO PASS AFTER MY FATHER HAD SPOKEN ALL THE WORDS OF HIS DREAM OR VISION, WHICH WERE MANY, HE SAID UNTO US, BECAUSE OF THESE THINGS WHICH HE SAW IN A VISION, HE EXCEEDINGLY FEARED FOR LAMAN AND LEMUEL; YEA, HE FEARED LEST THEY SHOULD BE CAST OFF FROM THE PRESENCE OF THE LORD.
BECAUSE OF THE THE THINGS WHICH I HAVE SEEN IN A VISION, I FEAR EXCEEDINGLY FOR LAMAN AND LEMUEL
AND HE DID EXHORT THEM THEN WITH ALL THE FEELING OF A TENDER PARENT, THAT THEY WOULD HEARKEN TO HIS WORDS, THAT PERHAPS THE LORD WOULD BE MERCIFUL TO THEM, AND NOT CAST THEM OFF;
HEARKEN UNTO MY WORDS, THAT THE LORD WILL BE MERCIFUL TO YOU AND NOT CAST YOU OFF.
YEA, MY FATHER DID PREACH UNTO THEM.
AND AFTER HE HAD PREACHED UNTO THEM, AND ALSO PROPHESIED UNTO THEM OF MANY THINGS, HE BADE THEM TO...
KEEP THE COMMANDMENTS OF THE LORD;
AND HE DID CEASE SPEAKING UNTO THEM. AND ALL THESE THINGS DID MY FATHER SEE, AND HEAR, AND SPEAK, AS HE DWELT IN A TENT, IN THE VALLEY OF LEMUEL,
AND ALSO A GREAT MANY MORE THINGS, WHICH CANNOT BE WRITTEN UPON THESE PLATES.

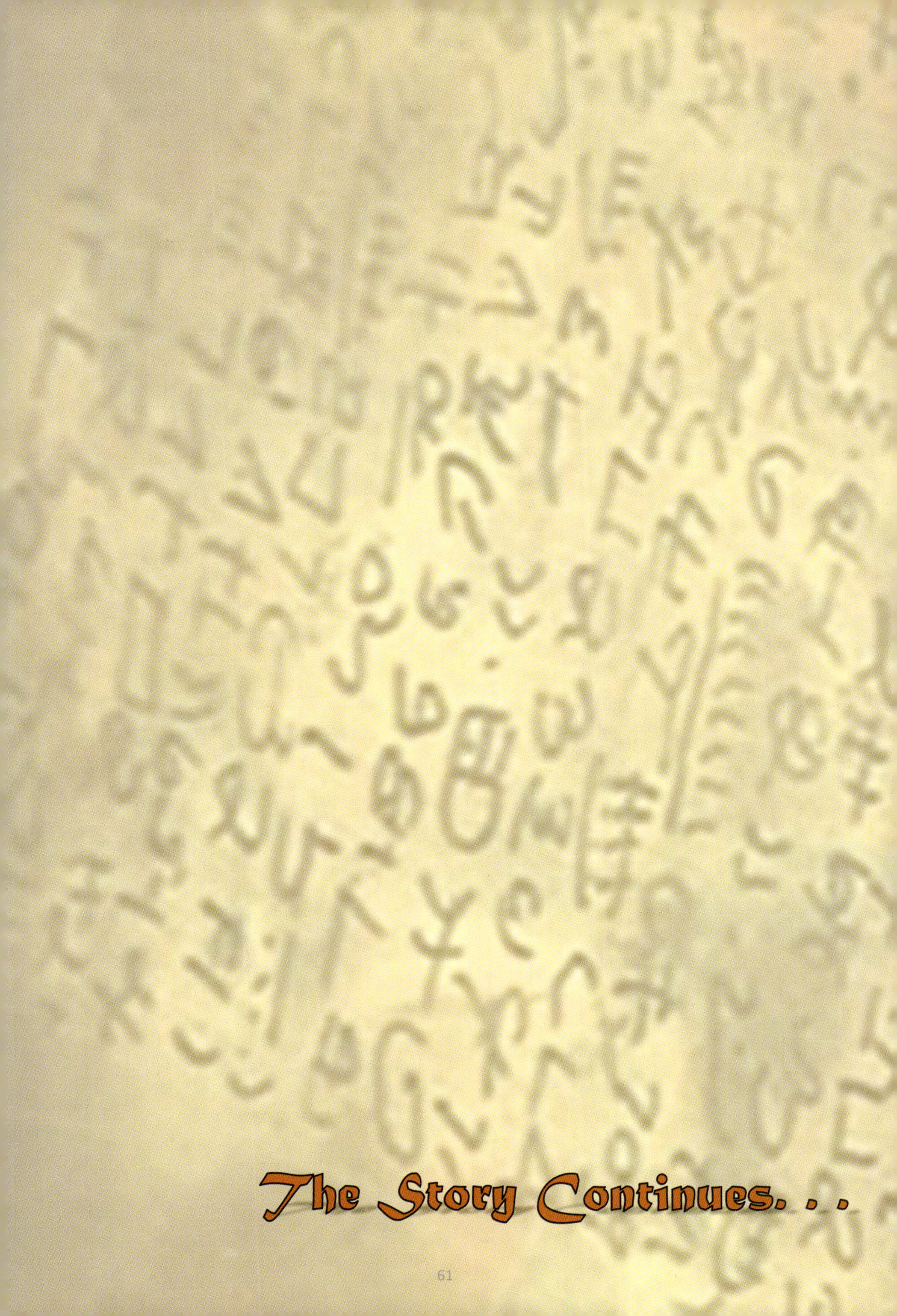

The Story Continues. . .

Don't Miss...

"To the Sea"

The next multi-chapter installment, covering 1 Nephi 15-17

Check out our website,
BookOfMormonComics.com
for more exciting updates

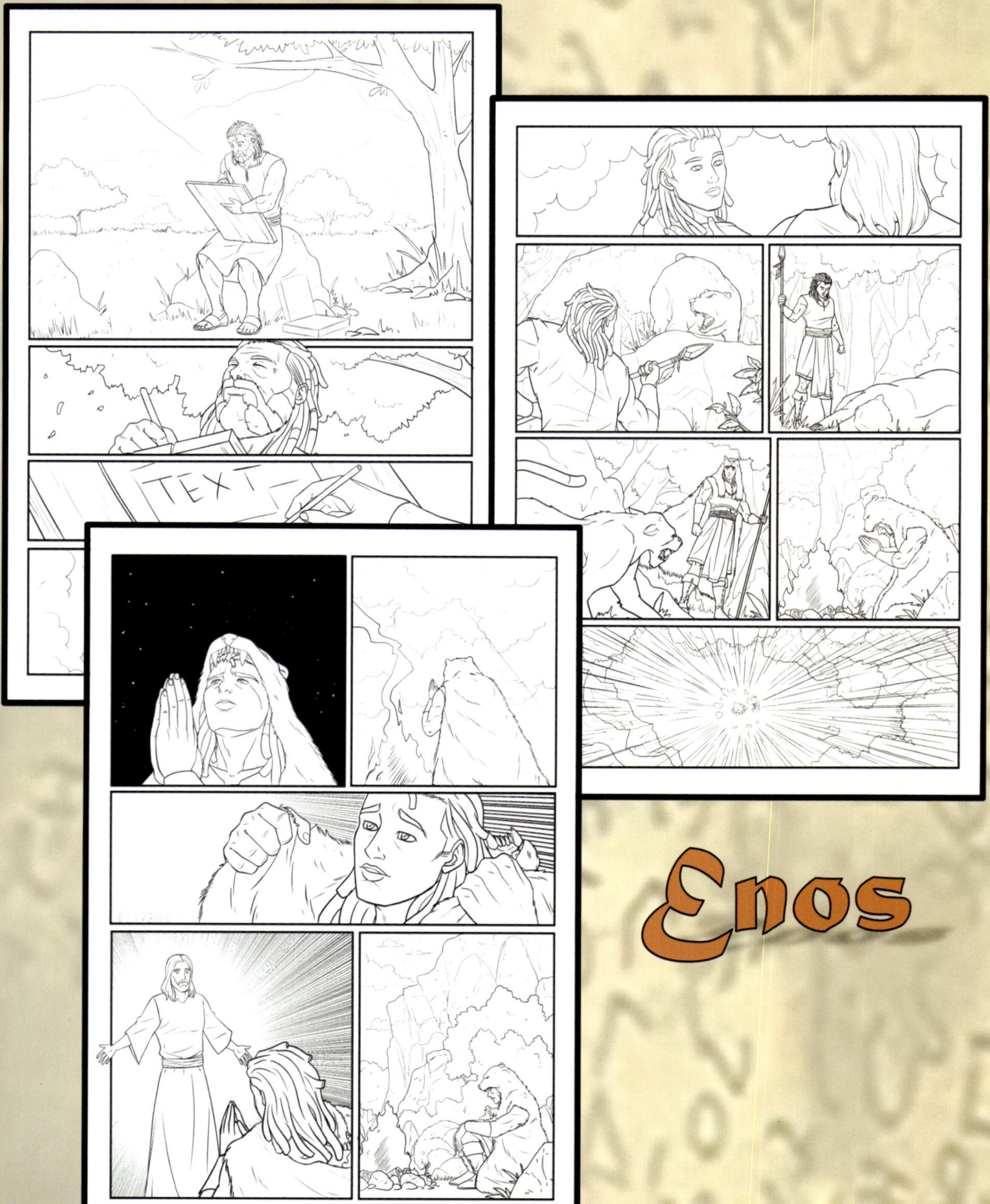

Enos

Jesus' Visit to America

Cover variant for Issue 2
based on chapter 5:
Sariah mourning the loss of her sons

Cover variant for Issue 2
based on chapter 8:
Lehi partakes of the fruit of the Tree of Life

While there are many who deserve thanks, we want to thank our earliest supporters, those that aided us financially when this comic was a thing "hoped for" and yet unseen.

A thousand thanks to our one and only

Angel Backer

Ben Arkell

A special thanks to those that showed the

Faith of Nephi

Mayrene Stewart
Patrick Malin
Donnie Appleman
Lara Jansson
Jessica Tessem
Robert Wickham
Kayley Kirkman
Adam Myers
Ashton

We asked them to join us and they

Went the Extra Mile

Craig T Powell
Patrick Salemme
Titanium
Theodore Barrett Burgin
Julie Ann Reid
Matt Alexander
Angela McPherson
Sarah Christensen
Chris
Cecilia Winkler

Thanks to those that believed in us

Enough to Share

Dai
Stacey Smith
Emma McCormick
Kevin Goodrich
Melanie Birch
Cindy Gritton

And thanks to everyone else

Who Believed

Joe Tippets
Shawn Jepson
Joshua Jay Carruth
Robyn Christensen
Christopher Bradford
Dominick Jarvis
Jared Miller
Lyndsey Dannenberg
David Glick
Denise Wallace
Megan Garner
Sherry Smart Saville
Tera Sweat
Conner Meacham
Adam K. K. Figueira
Jayson M.
Liz Busby
Michael J Sorensen
Nino Pingera
Thmazing
Natalie Edwards Ferguson
Kesten Harper
Andrew Stewart
Bradley Jackman
Christopher Davis
Holly Lucas
Colleen
Geoffrey
Max
Trevor Hawkins
Amy
Joah Fussell
Liz Kazandzhy
Norman Shurtliff
Benjamin Stewart
Mark Alldredge
Trent

To request permission, contact the publisher at Publisher@bookofmormoncomics.com

Hardcover: 978-1-7357592-0-3
Kickstarter Special Edition: 978-1-7357592-1-0

First published in 2020

Scripted by Michael W. Stewart
Studio work by WM Art Studio
Pencil and Inks by Daniele Sapuppo
Colors by Arianna Sabella
Lettering by Elisa Verçoza
Edited by Michel W. Stewart and Heather Collier
Cover Art by Katie Payne

Printed in P.R.C.

www.BookofMormonComics.com

Disclaimer: This work and all that belongs to it are the work of the artists and creators alone. This work was not produced by, nor does its art necessarily express the views of, The Church of Jesus Christ of Latter-day Saints (The Church). Efforts were made to be as historically accurate as possible. However, artistic license was also taken. At all times the artists and creators did their best to stay true to the text of The Book of Mormon.

Making the Cover

Art By Katie Payne